COVE NECK

COVE NECK

Oyster Bay's Historic Enclave

John E. Hammond & Elizabeth E. Roosevelt

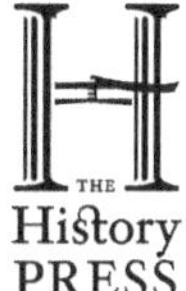

Published by The History Press
Charleston, SC
www.historypress.com

Front cover image of *Sagamore Hill* was taken by Elizabeth Emlen Roosevelt.
Back cover image of windmill at *Sagamore Hill* was taken by Elizabeth Emlen Roosevelt.

First published 2019

Manufactured in the United States

ISBN 9781467144377

Library of Congress Control Number: 2019945083

Notice: The information in this book is true and complete to the best of our knowledge. It is offered without guarantee on the part of the authors or The History Press. The authors and The History Press disclaim all liability in connection with the use of this book.

CONTENTS

Contents

Opposite: 1873 map of the north shore area of Long Island, showing Cove Neck nestled between Oyster Bay Harbor and Cold Spring Harbor. Except for the Smith's on the north end and the Swan brothers in the middle, the entire peninsula was used for farming. *Courtesy of Oyster Bay Historical Society.*

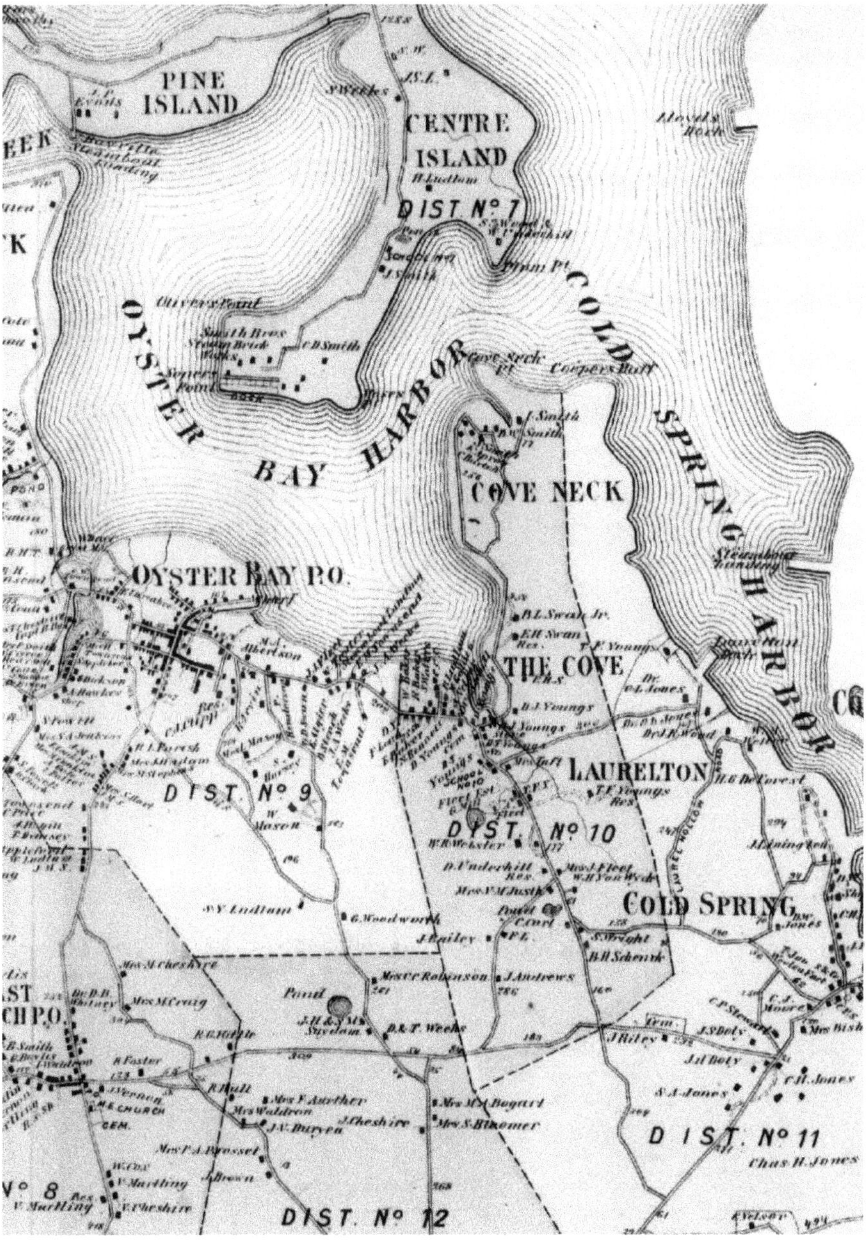

PINE ISLAND

CENTRE ISLAND

DIST. Nº 7

OYSTER BAY HARBOR

COLD SPRING HARBOR

COVE NECK

OYSTER BAY P.O.

THE COVE

LAURELTON

DIST. Nº 9

DIST. Nº 10

COLD SPRING

DIST. Nº 11

DIST. Nº 12

Nº 8

INTRODUCTION

More than a century ago, a New York newspaper referred to Cove Neck as the "Newport of New York." Cove Neck resident Theodore Roosevelt wrote of it in *The Outlook*, "There could be no healthier and pleasanter place in which to bring up children than in that nook of old-time America around *Sagamore Hill*." The founder of Vitagraph Studios, James Stuart Blackton, wrote in his autobiography that he and his wife, Paula, chose to live in Cove Neck because it was where "the Best People have their homes."

In her preface to *When We Were Little: Children's Rhymes of Oyster Bay*, Mary Fanny Youngs wrote about the Youngs family homestead, which still stands in Cove Neck today:

> *We lived in an old gray house…so close to the harbor that the high tides in the spring and autumn always flooded the dark, earth-floored cellar. For two hundred and sixty years the little old house has stood there and in all that time has never gone out of the possession of the lineal descendants of the stanch old pioneer who built it. For that reason, the love of the old traditions, the old ways, the very rafters over our heads and earth beneath our feet, were not only, "bred in our bone," they were soul of our souls.*

Theodore Roosevelt wrote of Cove Neck in his foreword to *When We Were Little: Children's Rhymes of Oyster Bay*, Mary Fanny's little book of poetry:

> *It is a lovely country....The people who dwelt on these farms or who got their livelihood on the waters of bay or Sound, came from a stock which had been on the island for nearly three centuries. The life was what they had themselves developed. They had no traditions of any other. Their roots had been in the soil for generations.*

Cove Neck is both the geographical name for the peninsula that extends from the southernmost part of Cold Spring Harbor and the political name for the entity that formed on it. When the Incorporated Village of Cove Neck was formed in 1927, the New York State law that was then in effect for incorporated villages limited their size to one square mile. As a result of this law, only the northern parts of the geographical Cove Neck became part of the Incorporated Village of Cove Neck.

This book tells the stories of the early days of the settlement in the 1600s and the difficulties of life in those early days, the hardships and struggles of Mary Cooper in the 1700s and the various transfers of property that led to the development of three major sections of land, which, by the early twentieth century, had become the Incorporated Village of Cove Neck.

1
FORMATION

When the first comprehensive history of New York was written in the 1830s, it was believed that Long Island was formed over countless millennia by the actions of the Atlantic Ocean, the Gulf Stream from the south and the Arctic currents from the north. When Munsell's *History of Queens County* was published in 1882, the formation of Long Island was described as having been the result of "the tides in the Atlantic, all combined to bring hither and deposit the materials of which this foundation consists." Modern science, however, tells us that Long Island was formed by the receding Wisconsin Glacier around twenty thousand years ago. The glacier, it is said, had pushed down, from New England, all the surface sands that form the north shore of Long Island and the glacial moraine that runs through the middle of the island. Over time, vegetation took root and ancient peoples began to settle there, perhaps as early as six thousand years ago.

An archaeological dig, completed in 1962 on the grounds of *Sagamore Hill*, confirmed that native peoples had used the area for encampments over a protracted period of time. Several exploratory digs in 1961 had uncovered an Indian hut foundation, and another excavation of the site revealed a rough, fieldstone foundation of a square hut with an area of about fifteen feet by fifteen feet and an entrance facing due south. The hut was fifty feet to the east of a stratified habitation area and was on the road that led to Mrs. Philip Roosevelt's beach house. The digs, which were done near Eel Creek, found several stone tools, including a triangular-stemmed

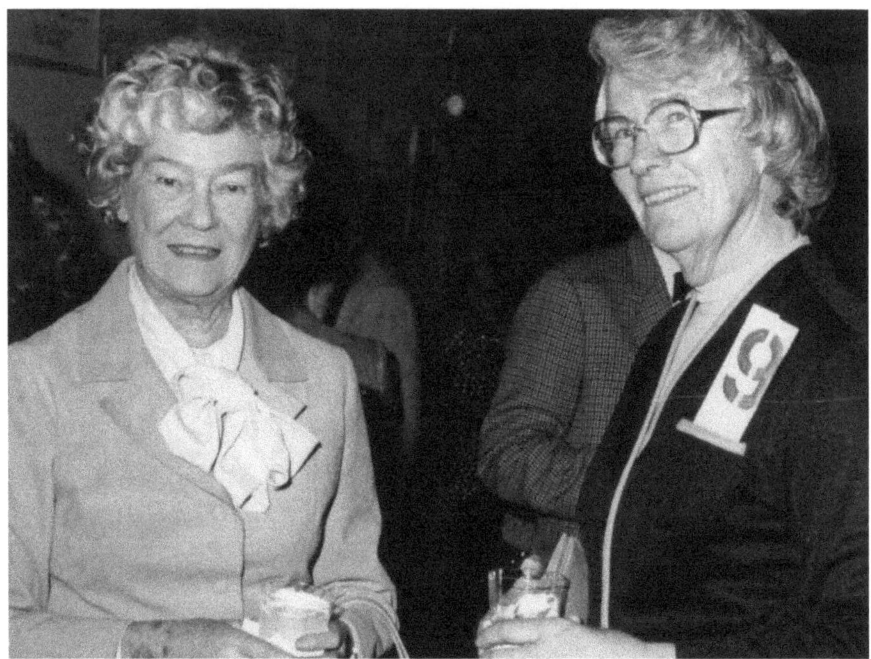

An archeological study along the west shore of Cold Spring Harbor discovered an Indian encampment. Frances Roosevelt, on the left, was the first historian of Cove Neck and made the discovery. Elizabeth Roosevelt, to the right, is the present historian of Cove Neck and coauthor of this book. *Courtesy John Hammond.*

black shale projectile, a black flint spear and a quartz hammer stone with areas indicating wear. There were also softshell clam ornaments and many shards of pottery. Frances Roosevelt, who had been appointed as the official historian for the Village of Cove Neck in April 1961, was credited with personally discovering the stone chipping site where the Native Americans turned stones into arrowheads. The conclusions of the study stated that the area was used as a campsite by a wide variety of Native American tribes over a considerable period of time.

At the time of the arrival of the first Europeans to the area, the only native peoples remaining in the area of Cove Neck were the Matinecocks. Matinecock means "at the hilly ground" and was the term used to describe the peoples who occupied the northern half of Long Island, from Flushing to Smithtown. The descriptive name appears quite appropriate, as their territory followed the glacial moraine, which traverses the middle of Long Island. The Matinecocks were part of the greater Algonquin language and cultural group, but they never had any written language. They were described as hunter-gatherers who subsisted on fishing, hunting and small fields of corn, or *maize*, as they called it. By the time of the arrival of the first Europeans, around the early 1600s, the total population of the thirteen chieftaincies on Long Island was about 6,500, and only a portion of that number were Matinecocks. The European arrival drastically reduced these numbers, as the diseases of the Europeans ravaged the native population, who had no internal resistance to them. Daniel Denton, while writing about Long Island in 1670, said that the demise of the Native Americans was due to divine intervention: "It hath been generally observed that where the English come to settle, a Divine Hand makes way for them, by removing or cutting off the Indians either by Wars one with the other, or by some raging mortal disease." By 1685, the last native-owned land had been acquired by the Europeans, and by 1709, only small, isolated remnants of the Matinecock tribe remained.

2

EARLY SETTLEMENT OF THE NORTH SIDE

The earliest surviving Oyster Bay town record, aside from the original purchase deed of 1653, was referred to as the *Book of Purposes*. In 1868, Jacob T. Bowne of Glen Cove placed a new cover on the old book. The first two pages of the *Book of Purposes* were lost sometime prior to 1868, which makes page three the earliest surviving page. Page three mentions several purchases of land and buildings made by John Richbell in and around Oyster Bay in December 1660. A few pages later, the book says, "John Richbell have taken up ten acares of land the norte end of cove neck lying east and wast December the one & twentieth Day 1660."

John Richbell was born in Hampshire, England, around 1616; his father, John Richbell, was a merchant. The exact date of his coming to the New World is not recorded, but he can be found in records from Charlestown, Massachusetts, in 1648. On September 30, 1649, he was recorded in Antego (Antigua) as a witness to the will of William Homes. In 1657, his location was recorded on St. Christopher's Island in the West Indies. The noted nineteenth-century New England genealogist James Savage wrote of Richbell, "He seems to have married, while on one of his visits to the West Indies, Mistress Ann Parsons of St. Christopher's." Others have placed the time of that marriage in 1651.

In October 1651, the Cromwell government in England passed the first of several bills referred to as the Navigation Acts. The intent of these bills was to exclude the Dutch, who at that time dominated European trade, from any direct trade with England or its colonies. The Navigation Acts

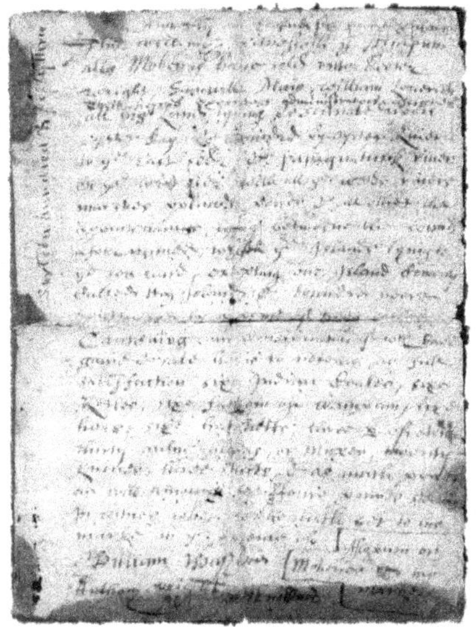

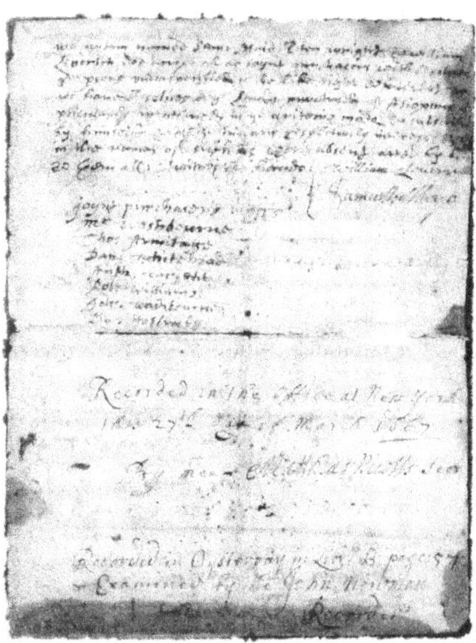

Left: 1653 deed of purchase for Oyster Bay, signed by Samuel Mayo, William Leverich and Peter Wright. Cove Neck determined the eastern boundary of the purchase. *Courtesy of the Town of Oyster Bay.*

Right: The reverse side of the 1653 deed of purchase contains the signatures of additional purchasers. The deed was recorded in New York by the colonial governor, Matthias Nicholls, in 1667. *Courtesy of the Town of Oyster Bay.*

prohibited foreign ships from transporting goods into or out of England or its colonies. The Navigation Acts had a significant impact on entrepreneurs like John Richbell and his partners, who had become involved in making annual trading voyages to the West Indies. Richbell became involved with shipments to England, the West Indies and the English colonies in modern New England. On one of his annual voyages, prior to 1656, he entered into a business arrangement in Barbados with Thomas Modiford, also of Hampshire, England, and William Sharpe.

The following year, John Richbell's partners, Modiford and Sharpe, wrote instructions to him from Barbados on September 18, 1657. They instructed him to establish connections with those who controlled the governments of the lands between Connecticut and the Dutch colony of New Amsterdam and to learn about their standings with the Native Americans. They advised him to purchase a small plantation there near a navigable river and on land that was well watered and well wooded, but they warned him to be very sure that the title was clear so that he did not involve them in legal disputes. His partners were especially concerned about the Dutch and their claims to the land. They closed the letter with a strong warning: "Lastly, we desire you to advise us or either of us how affairs stand with you, what your wants are and how they may be most advantageously employed by us, for the life of our business will consist in the nimble, quiet and full correspondence with us."

The last sentence of the directive to John Richbell raises questions about the true nature of the business activities of him and his partners. What did they mean by "nimble, quiet and full correspondence?" Did their business activities require them to circumnavigate the Navigation Acts recently passed by the English Parliament? Were they involved in piracy? The area around Oyster Bay, which included Cove Neck, was then a disputed territory between the Dutch and the English. Because of this contention, Oyster Bay became a center for illegal activity, including piracy and a great deal of smuggling, during this time. In spring 1699, William Kidd was returned to Oyster Bay Harbor to face possible piracy charges; some rumors say that he sent some of his men ashore to bury some of his pirate "booty" on Centre Island or on Cove Neck. One of Kidd's men was believed to be Jacob Conklin of Huntington, who had signed on with Captain Kidd in September 1696. When Kidd and his crew landed at Oyster Bay in 1699, Conklin disembarked from the ship and never went back, so Kidd left Oyster Bay without him. None of the supposed buried treasure was ever found on Centre Island or on Cove Neck, and Jacob Conklin was married shortly after Kidd's execution in London in 1701. Later, Conklin reportedly bought up much of the property in and around Huntington township and died a wealthy man in 1754.

Another possibility is that Richbell and his partners were involved in the slave trade. Their business activities in Barbados involved sugar, which was in high demand for the making of rum, and at the time, the production of sugar required hard labor from a large number of slaves, which would imply that they were also involved in the slave trade. The Portuguese had settled Barbados early in the seventeenth century and began bringing enslaved people from Africa to work the sugar cane fields. Many of these Portuguese slave traders were Sephardic Jews who also owned large sugar plantations in Recife, Brazil. In 1654, the Sephardic Jews were thrown out of Recife and sought transport on a ship bound for Europe. In 1654, twenty-three Jews arrived in New Amsterdam from Recife after their ship was captured by Spanish pirates, who were then taken over by the crew of the *Saint Charles*, a French ship that was on its way to New Amsterdam. These refugees established a small Jewish settlement in New Amsterdam, but they

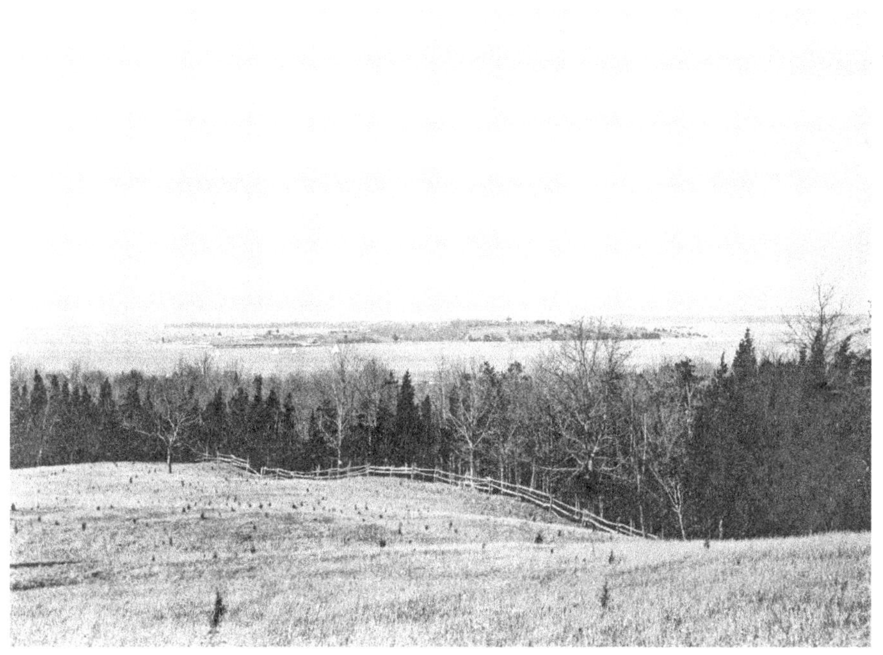

Centre Island as it appeared in the 1800s, when this photo was taken. Cove Neck is to the right. *Courtesy of the Oyster Bay Historical Society.*

were unable to openly practice their faith. Although the Dutch West India Company had granted a Charter of Freedoms and Exemptions in 1640, which granted some tolerances, only members of the Dutch Reformed Church could practice their faith publicly. Peter Styvesant, the director of the West India Company of Amsterdam, strongly disliked Jews, which resulted in the denial of their numerous petitions seeking leniency. By the 1720s, the Jewish population had grown in New Amsterdam, and efforts were started to build a synagogue, which was completed on Mill Street in Manhattan and named Shearith Israel. Nathan Simpson kept detailed records of the congregation members, and his records show that Moses Levy, Jacob Franks and Nathan Simson were part of the majority, the Ashkenazim, although the congregation followed the rituals of the minority, the Sephardim. Levy, Franks and Simson all had connections to Oyster Bay and Cove Neck. Jacob Franks owned a considerable amount of land in Oyster Bay, and he ran the following ad in the *New York Weekly Journal* from April to June 1743: "To be sold on Reasonable terms, A large dwelling house two stories high sash windows with ten acres of orchard adjoining to said house and four acres of meadow before the door being in Town of Oyster Bay on Long Island." This is believed to have been the building next to Raynham Hall, which was bought by Jacob Townsend, the brother of Samuel Townsend of Raynham Hall. The Jacob Townsend building was torn down in 1900.

Bilhah Abigail Levy was born on November 26, 1696, in London, England, and married Jacob Franks, who had been a boarder with her father, Moses Levy. Jacob Franks became very wealthy through supplying food, clothing and ammunition to British colonial forces and through the slave trade. In a letter to her son, Naphtali, who had moved to London, Bilhah related how her daughter, Richea, had "been out of town this three weeks at Huntington and Oyster Bay." Edith B. Gells wrote in a footnote in her book, *The Letters of Abigail Levy Franks,* "Joseph Simson, a noted merchant made freeman on February1, 1743, owned considerable land in Oyster Bay with his wife Rebecca Isaacs Simson. Since Richea returned with the Simsons, she may have been visiting them. The Frankses and Simsonses seem to be the first Jews owning property in the Oyster Bay area." Joseph Simson, the nephew of Nathan Simson, owned property at the Fresh Pond, near the property of Tom Gall at the foot of Moore's Hill Road, which was in the geographic Cove Neck but not included in the political Cove Neck. Joseph Simson owned a ten-acre parcel near the home of Joseph Youngs in Cove Neck and was a merchant importer and exporter. Joseph's uncle, Nathan Simson, was a large merchant trader, slave trader and a partner in various ventures with Jacob Franks and his wife, Abigail Levy Franks.

As mentioned earlier, John Richbell bought land on the northern end of Cove Neck in December 1660. He also bought the property of Daniel Whitehead, which contained a dwelling house, and acquired other prior purchases of others who had bought property on Cove Neck directly from the Native Americans. By the middle of the 1660s, Richbell had settled in Mamaroneck and began to sell off his properties in Oyster Bay and Cove Neck. At this time, John Richbell also owned all of Horse Neck (present-day Lloyd's Neck), which he had bought from Samuel Andrews. His right of ownership of Horse Neck was challenged by John Conkling from Huntington, who was supported by the freeholders of Huntington. The case was tried, and the jury in the Court of Assizes ruled in favor of Conkling, however, when the court looked further into the case, it reversed its ruling, saying that "it was determined that Horseneck doth of righ belong to John Richbell and his heirs." This decision was reinforced by a directive from the colonial governor, Richard Nicolls. On June 23, 1665, Richbell signed an agreement that said Horse Neck was officially a part of Oyster Bay.

On November 17, 1666, Richbell sold his large property holdings on Cove Neck to Latamore Sampson, but the town freeholders were not at all pleased with the sale. The freeholders stewed over the transaction for some time before they finally agreed to issue a legal protest against the sale:

> *Wharas Mr. John Richbell, hath made A Deede of Sale, unto one* [Latamore] *Sampson, of Seaverall percels, of lands within ye bounds, of our Towne, of Oyster Bay, wee ye Towne of Oyster Bay, for good, Considerations, moveing us theare unto, doe make our Leagall protest, against, ye Deede of Sale, which Mr. Richbell, hath made unto ye A for said* [Latamore] *Sampson: Oyster Bay ye last of July 1669.*

The debate over the Latamore Sampson property was resolved when the original agreement between the Town of Oyster Bay and Latamore Sampson was amended and confirmed.

> *Itt is Agreed yt* [Latamore] *Sampson in Lew of one fifteenth off Cove neck bought of John Richbill, he shall have three hundred Accars of Land, and one hundred Accars for his twenty Accars A Lott for five Lotts Viz, out on ye End of Cove neck, he to give up to ye towne his five Accare Lott by Anthony wrights, and in Case A Convenyant place falls out to fence though it be forty Accars less hee to be Contented wittnes my hand.* [Latamore] *Sampson.*

Latamore Sampson was a wealthy young Englishman who had been a partner of Nathaniel Sylvester of Shelter Island and was engaged to Sylvester's eldest daughter, Grissel. Nathaniel Sylvester had been a slave trader, which was perhaps the reason for the displeasure of the Oyster Bay freeholders at the sale of John Richbell's property to him. Sampson held on to his property at Cove Neck until November 9, 1674, when he wrote it into his will. He was intending to make a trip to Barbados, and knowing the dangers of such a trip, he prepared his will, naming his partner and fiancée as executors of his will. Sampson's will also listed Grissel as the sole beneficiary of all of his properties. Latamore Sampson's will was probated on February 18, 1675. Whether or not Sampson died on the trip to Barbados is unknown. Some researchers believe that Sampson died of consumption before marrying Grissel. After Sampson's death, Grissel married James Lloyd of Boston, who became the owner of the Latamore Sampson property. Following the death of Nathaniel Sylvester in 1680, his attorney, Thomas Hartt, negotiated the sale of the property to Simon Cooper of Shrewsbury, New Jersey.

3

THE COOPER PROPERTY

Simon Cooper was born in London, England, where he became a distinguished chirurgeon (surgeon) before coming to America and settling in Shrewsbury, New Jersey. Simon Cooper wanted to buy the Latamore Sampson land on the north end of Cove Neck, but he also wanted the debate over the property to be resolved before he purchased the land. The surveyors appointed by the Town of Oyster Bay then went about their work and reported that the land was bounded by Fishing Creek on the west side of Cove Neck and by Eel Creek around the northeast end of Cove Neck. Their determination was short ten acres of the four hundred acres Cooper had agreed upon. In order to remedy this situation, the surveyors added the following:

> *Acording to Agrement between latemore sampson and ye towne, have Consented & Agreed to laye out to Simon Cooper ten Acres of land Elce whare upon ye towne comans which is to be in full Consideration of ye first Agrement between ye towne and Latemore Sampson, witness our hands on ye other side—Itt tis to be understood that ye sayd simon Cooper is to have, all the Creeks Coves and marshes within ye sayd bounds of Cove neck as by us marked to highwatter mark as wittnes oure hands with free liberty of A watter fence for Ever to secuar his lands.* [Dated January 30, 1682].

The agreement was then ratified by the freeholders of the town:

> *The Abovesaid order of ye Constable and oversears and ye Agrement of* [Latamore] *Sampson with ye towne As Above Exspressed, is Excepted byy ye towne, and Agreed to be layd out to Simon Cooper As proper right, by A free voat of ye towne at A towne metting held this 27th of Jenewary 1682 this is to be understood ye four hundred Accars granted to* [Latamore] *Sampson Abovesayd This Entred by order of the towne by me Tho: Townsend Recorder.*

Upon the death of Simon Cooper, sometime prior to 1691, his widow, Mary (or Martha), on February 29, 1692, passed the 400 acres at Cove Neck on to her son Robert Cooper (born February 1700), with the full agreement of Robert's older brother, Simon (born April 1694). Robert passed on the land by his will, in 1718, to his brother Joseph Cooper (born 1705). Joseph kept about 242 acres of the land and left the rest of the 400-acre plot to Robert's older brother Simon Cooper and Robert's cousin, who was also named Simon Cooper. Joseph Cooper married Mary Wright (born May 18, 1714), the daughter of William Wright and Elizabeth Rhodes, on May 22, 1729.

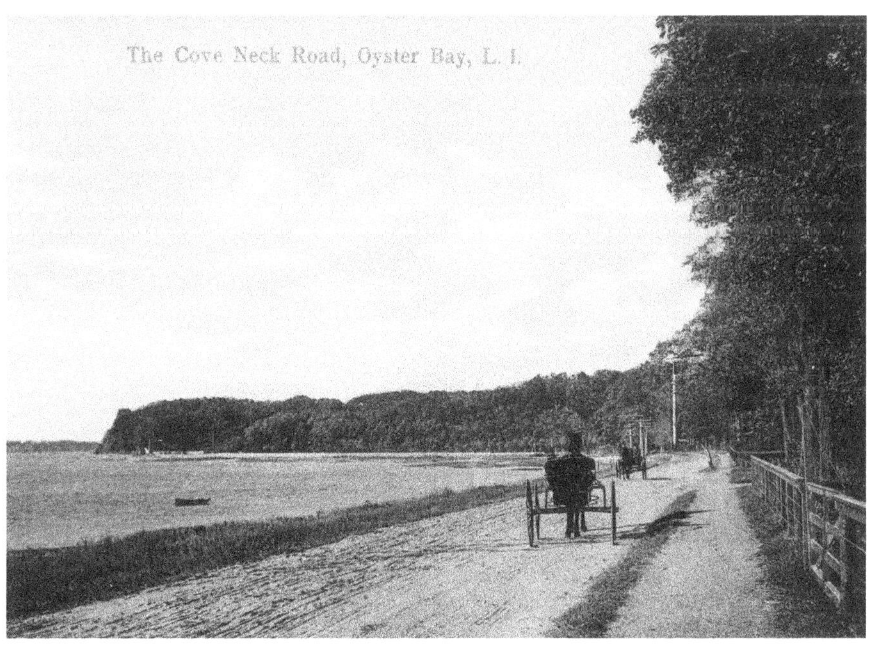

Cove Neck Road was unpaved until the early twentieth century. *Courtesy John Hammond.*

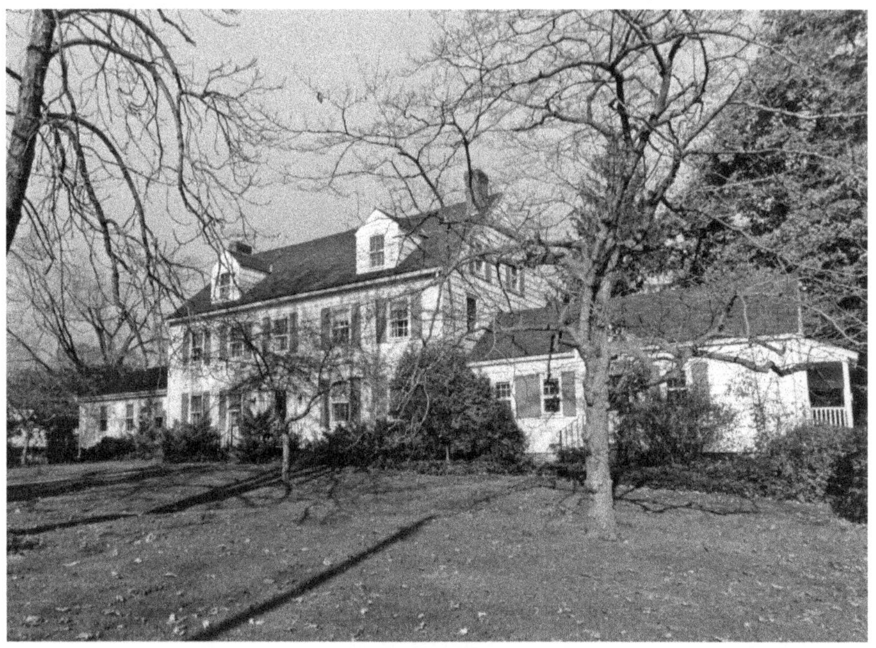

Mary Wright was born in this house, which was built by her father, William Wright, in 1705. The house survives to this day on West Main Street. *Courtesy John Hammond.*

From 1768 to 1773, Mary Cooper kept a diary telling of the travails of eighteenth-century farm life on Cove Neck. In the introduction to *The Diary of Mary Cooper*, which was published by the Oyster Bay Historical Society, Field Horne wrote, "Mary's diary is the only such document surviving from the New York colonial period written by a woman, and one of the very few written by a woman in any American colony. As a record of farm life of that period, it is unique." Mary Wright married Joseph Cooper at St. George's Church in Hempstead just one week after her fifteenth birthday; Joseph Cooper was a few days shy of his twenty-fourth birthday. Forty years later, she wrote in her diary, "This day is forty years sinc I left my father's house and come here, and here I have seene little els but harde labour and sorrow, crosses of every kind. I think in every respect the state of my affairs is more then forty times worse then when I came here first, except that I am nearer the desierered haven." Mary had seen all of her six children die; two as infants, two as very young children and two as adults. At the time of her death, she was survived by only one grandchild, Sarah (Sally), to whom her husband, Joseph Cooper, left everything.

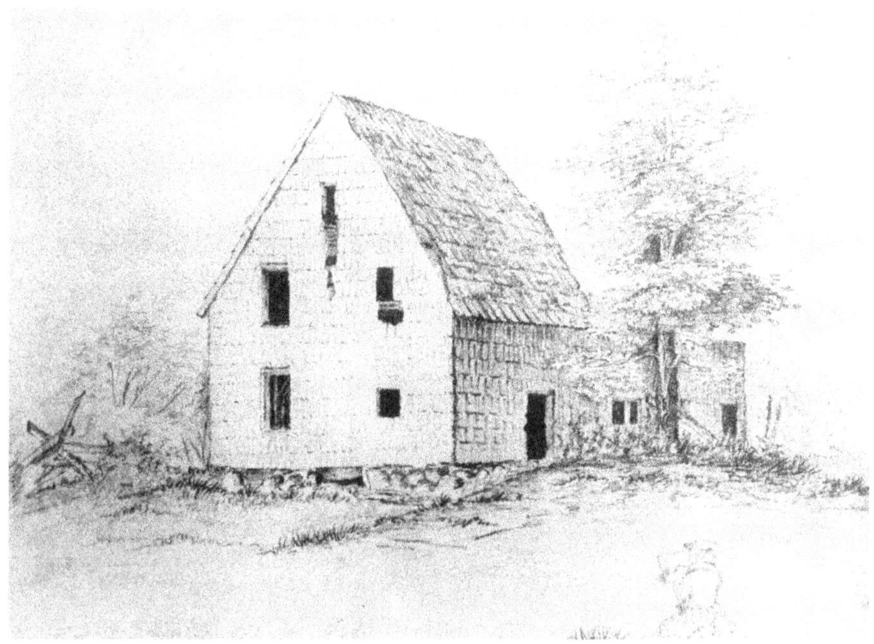

The Cooper house was originally smaller than it is today. *Courtesy Oyster Bay Historical Society.*

Mary Cooper's oldest daughter, Elizabeth Ann, was born on June 30, 1734, at Cove Neck. Against her mother's wishes, Elizabeth Ann (Bet Ann) eloped with Dr. Thomas Wright, her cousin, in 1751. After the marriage, Mary severed all contact with Bet Ann. There was never a reconciliation between the two until Bet Ann died four years later, in 1755, leaving her daughter in the care of her mother, who took her in and raised as her own. Mary Cooper had Bet Ann's body brought to the Coopers' home on Cove Neck and insisted that it be carried into the house through the same window that Bet Ann had left when she eloped. When the funeral was held, Bet Ann's body was taken out of the house through the front door and taken to the Baptist Church Cemetery in Oyster Bay for burial.

Mary Cooper got little satisfaction from her other daughter, Esther, who also married her first cousin, Simon Cooper, on April 19, 1762, just after her eighteenth birthday. On April 14, 1769, Mary wrote that Esther had gone away on some business and "our people quriel with her and Semon Cooper turned her out of doors and threw her over the fence to my greate grief and sorrow." On July 16, 1769, Mary recorded, "Simon Cooper is making some proposels to live with Ester." A few months later, on October

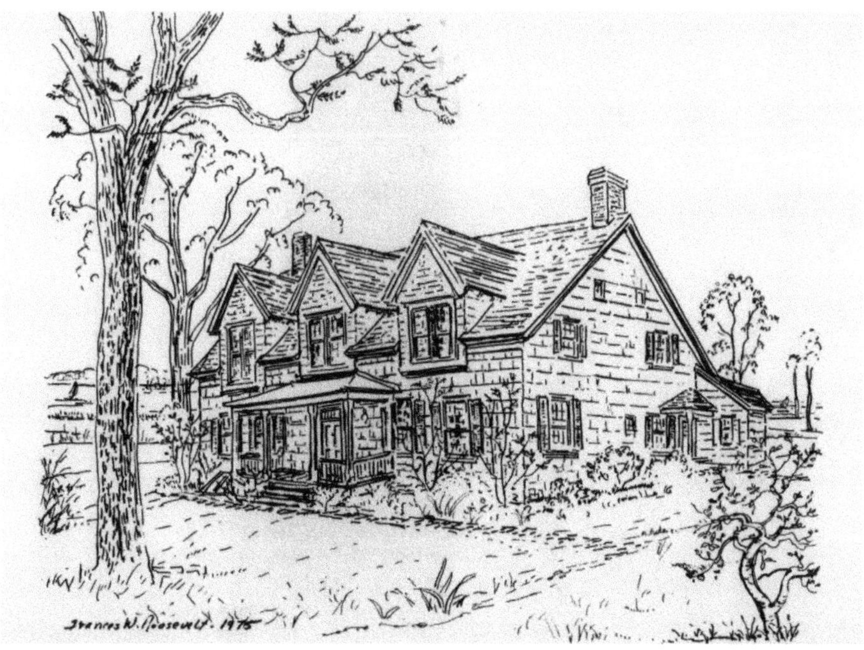

Frances Roosevelt made this contemporary drawing of the Molly Cooper House. *Courtesy of the Oyster Bay Historical Society.*

1, 1769, Mary wrote, "Simon Cooper quarrel very greately about Ester dancing. He got in a unxpresabel rage and struck her." Mary Cooper mentions Esther frequently in her diary and tells of Esther's struggles with depression. She said her daughter would sometimes cry continually for a week or more.

Mary relates in her diary the many nights she would stay up very late, sometimes without sleeping at all, to dry apples and pears. During her days on the farm, Mary prepared and preserved food, cleaned the house, washed dishes and clothes and engaged in the domestic production of thread, soap and candles. Overwork was a constant problem for women during this period, as all domestic work was performed by them. Mary wrote often about her depressed state.

Situated as it was on the tip of Cove Neck, the Cooper house was a stopping point for all manner of visitors, although it was never designated an inn. Mary's most detested visitors were Ben Hildreth and his friends, who brought along their two dogs, which they kept at the dining table, much to Mary's displeasure. She wrote that she was "much freted by them and their two dogs which they keep att table and in the bed room with them. The first I herde this morning was Ben's dogs barking and yeling in the bed room." Mary also griped that the men "did nothing but drink themselves drunk all the day long and sent for more rum." She constantly complained about the large numbers of visitors she had to tend to and provide meals for. On one occasion, Mary wrote, "O, I am tired almost to death waiteing on visseters. My feet ach as if the bones was laid bare. Not one day's rest have I had this weeke. I have no time to take care of my clothes or even to think my thoughts."

Mary occasionally got some respite from her daily toils. It was during these times that she would occasionally go to a frolic, as they were called. Frolics were gatherings, of various sorts, done by a group, much like a modern quilting bee. Mary's main relief was her deep religious conviction; however, she was in a constant search for meaning. She wrote about attending the various meetings of the Friends, Anglicans, Baptists and New Lights, which all had meetinghouses in Oyster Bay. Mary had been raised in the Anglican tradition but married into a Quaker family. She became an active Baptist at the Oyster Bay Baptist Church until there was a split in the group and the New Lights were formed. Her sister, Sarah Wright, who had married John Townsend, was an adherent of the New Lights Baptist Church, which was led by Reverend Peter Underhill, the son-in-law of Sarah Townsend. Getting

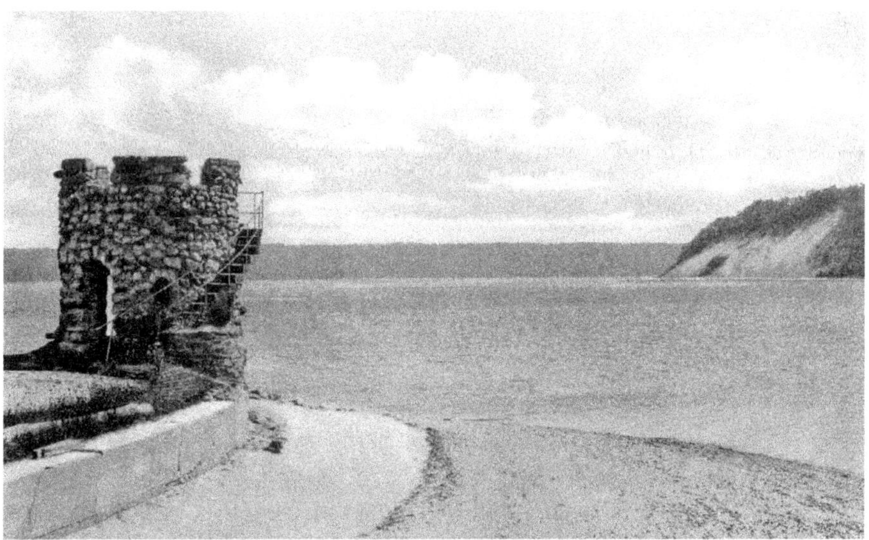

Cooper's Bluff is a prominent landmark on the northernmost point of Cove Neck. This photo, taken from Centre Island, shows Cooper's Bluff on the right. Members of the Roosevelt family enjoyed jumping off the top of the bluff. *Courtesy John Hammond.*

to the meetings was sometimes a chore for Mary, as she had to cross over the Cove Brook, which ran down from Arnold Fleet's Mill to the Brook House, as it was called by the Youngs family. At the best of times, crossing the creek only took a small hop, but the waters were frequently high, resulting in a long walk around the brook to find a crossable spot. In winter, it was perilous to cross the creek, as the ice and snow made the trek more difficult. Mary wrote several times of falling into the brook.

Mary Cooper wrote her diary until sometime after October 1773, where surviving pages become unreadable and others have been lost. Mary died on August 22, 1778, and like other members of her family, she was buried in the Baptist Church Cemetery in Oyster Bay. Her husband, Joseph Cooper, died a few months later on November 15, 1778, and was buried alongside her.

Sarah Wright, the only surviving descendant of Joseph and Mary Cooper and sole recipient of the Cooper estate, married Justus Storrs on May 2, 1788. After their marriage, Justus Storrs sold the 262-acre property to Thomas Smith of Hog Island (Centre Island). Thomas Smith willed the property to his son, Thomas, on October 6, 1793, who then passed the land on to his son, Abraham. Abraham was considered peculiar and subject to childish whims by his family. He was amply provided for in his father's will, and his brother Thomas was designated to inherit the family's homestead on Centre Island. However, Thomas's wife, Deborah Butler, had a dislike for the separation of Centre Island from Oyster Bay, where her family lived. At that time, travel was difficult across the bay, and to travel by land was considered tedious. Arrangements were made for an exchange between Thomas and Jacob, and the arrangement was completed on February 6, 1818. The North Side holdings of the Smith family remained undeveloped for most of the nineteenth century. Some of the Smith family holdings on Cove Neck were acquired by Sarah (Sally) Smith, a daughter of William Wallace Smith and granddaughter of Daniel White Smith, who was born on March 4, 1872, married Ernest Hutchinson and died on August 10,

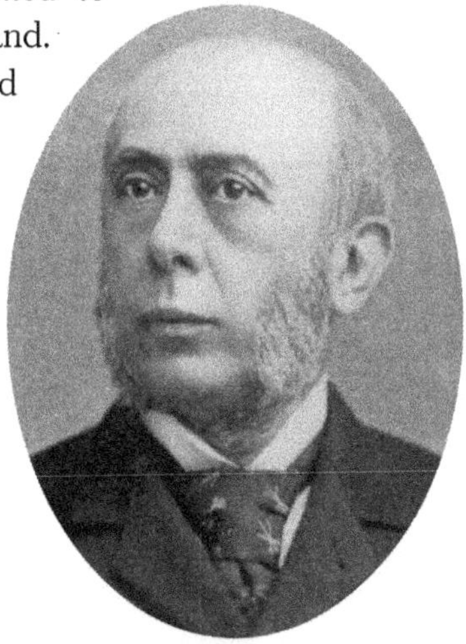

Frederic Coudert bought one of the thirty-acre parcels from the Smith family and built his summer home. *Courtesy of the Oyster Bay Historical Society.*

1899. After Sally's death, the Hutchinsons sold off a sizable portion of their property to Walter Starr, who was seeking to mine Cooper's Bluff for its sand. The Hutchinsons did retain a portion of the land, and the family continued to own the property throughout the twentieth century. Lena Cock Smith, another daughter of Daniel Smith and sister of Sally Smith Hutchinson, also acquired some of the property at Cove Neck on the north end, but she did not live there. Lena lived on Park Avenue in New York City and had a home on the south fork of Long Island.

The Smith family met to divide the remaining 150 acres still held by the family into five 30-acre parcels to be sold, which they valued at $1,000 per acre. One of the first purchasers of the land was Walter D. Starr, president of the Long Island Sand Company, who purchased a 30-acre tract that included Cooper's Bluff. Starr sought permission from the Oyster Bay Town Board to construct a sand dock at Coopers Bluff in the summer of 1900. Several residents stepped forward in opposition to Starr's proposal, including Theodore Roosevelt. Starr's opponents tried to enlist the assistance of the Army Corps of Engineers through the War Department, but the corps would not get involved, stating that it had no jurisdiction. The case was bitterly fought by residents and property owners of Cove Neck and Centre Island until, finally, Walter Starr sold the property in October 1901 to a syndicate of property developers headed by Charles W. Wetmore. Wetmore had settled on Centre Island a decade earlier and built his 60-acre estate there named *Applegate*.

Frederic R. Coudert and his wife, Alys Tracy Wilmerding, purchased one of the 30-acre parcels, as did their son-in-law, Frederick Benedict, and Frank C. Swan. Other purchasers of these parcels included Robert W. Gibson and Howard Caswell Smith, who would become the first mayor when the village became incorporated in 1927.

4

YOUNGS HOMESTEAD AND SETTLEMENT OF THE SOUTH SIDE

One of the oldest surviving structures in Cove Neck is the Youngs Homestead. Tradition says that it was built sometime in the 1660s. This date comes from a family history, the *Youngs Record,* written by Daniel Kelsey Youngs and privately printed in 1890. A few years earlier, Daniel had written the agricultural section of Munsell's *1882 History of Queens County*, which contained a biographical sketch of him. This was perhaps his motivation for researching and preparing the *Youngs Record*. In the history, Daniel sought to establish, through surviving documents, when the Youngs family first came to Oyster Bay. Based on his research, he claimed that the Youngs family settled in Oyster Bay even before the first purchase settlers arrived in 1653.

Thomas Youngs was the progenitor of the Youngs family of Oyster Bay. He was a son of Captain Joseph Youngs and a grandson of Reverend Christopher Youngs. Daniel Kelsey Youngs placed Thomas Youngs's birth in 1625 in Southwold, England. However, Daniel confused the Thomas Youngs born in 1625 with his cousin of the same name, who was the actual progenitor, born around 1645 in Southold, Long Island. This mistake was discovered in a later and more authoritative history of the Youngs family done by Selah Youngs Jr., which was privately printed in 1907. Regarding the Thomas Youngs born in 1625, Selah wrote, "He wrote his name both Young and Yongs, and has been confounded with Thomas Youngs of Oyster Bay, L.I., who was his cousin."

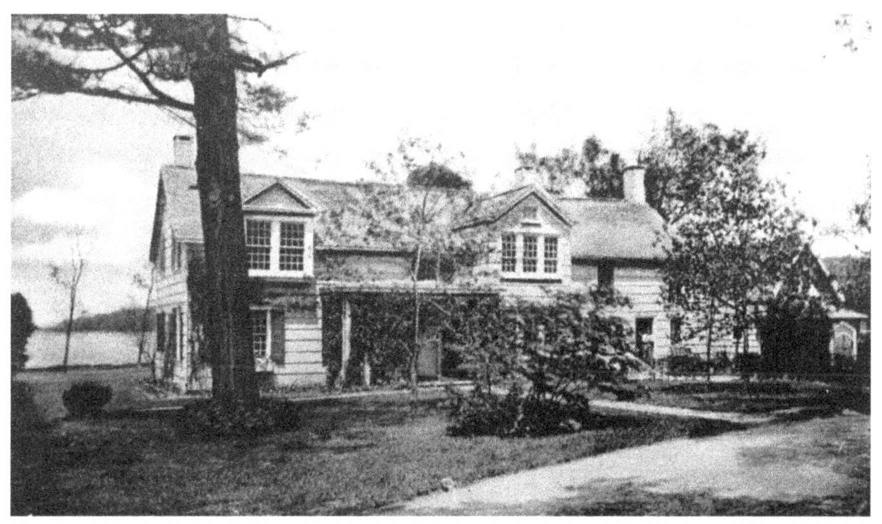

The original parts of the Youngs Homestead were built around 1676. The family retained ownership of the property until William Jones Youngs died in 1916. *Courtesy John Hammond.*

In the *Youngs Record*, Daniel wrote that Thomas Youngs "removed to Oyster Bay, date not known." Later in the same work, he wrote, "There is no record or reliable authority for the date of his coming to Oyster Bay." A Thomas Young is first mentioned in the records as a witness to the sale of a slave, Owah, who came to be known as Black Tom, dated November 26, 1673. However, it is not clear from the record that this is the same Thomas Young who later settled in Oyster Bay. This was possibly the Thomas Youngs who was given a grant of land at Greenwich, Connecticut, on October 4, 1673.

The date of Thomas Youngs's settling in Oyster Bay is established by a grant of land given to him at a town meeting on December 9, 1676, where it is recorded:

> *Given at ye Same meeting unto Thomas Youngs three Acres of Land for a home Lott Lying on ye Side of ye Cove Neck Swamp ye rear Joyning to ye Land William Buckler bought of John Dickason and fronting Northwest to ye highway at ye head of ye Cove with free Commonage of grassing and timber provided that ye Sd Thomas Youngs Doth buld upon ye Sd Lot or fence it within a Twelve month and a day if not ye Sd Lot and Commons is to return to ye Town again without Exception.*

It is also clear from the record that he did in fact build within the specified time period, as he is accepted as a Freeholder and allotted a right in Unkeway Neck in 1679; he sold this right at Unkeway Neck to his father-in-law, Richard Harcutt, the following year. This firmly establishes the date of the building of the Youngs Homestead as between December 9, 1676, and December 9, 1677.

It is clear from the writings of Daniel Kelsey Youngs that he had access to and was aware of the preceding documents, since he cites them in his writing. Nevertheless, he determined the arrival of his ancestor Thomas Youngs in Oyster Bay much earlier based upon a family lease of property, which was found in a group of records collected by his son, William Jones Youngs. He wrote of Thomas Youngs, "The date of his first coming to Oyster Bay is fixed with tolerable accuracy, by documentary evidence.... His first signature to any document preserved, is attached to a lease of his farm, to two of his sons, in 1670." Daniel goes on to copy the entire lengthy document into his book. The lease, as quoted in the *Youngs Record,* is dated at, "Oyster Bay, the first month, twentieth day, 1670." In the agreement, Thomas Youngs agrees to lease his farm to his two sons, Thomas and Richard, and goes on in detail to state the terms of the lease, which is to run for three and a half years. One of the terms stated, "They are to have two thirds of the fruit, and I reserve one or two barrels for John Youngs, and so every year following as they enjoy it."

Daniel determined that the fruit in question was apples when he wrote, "He had raised a sufficient number of apple trees to anticipate a production of several barrels." Youngs then went on to establish the arrival date of Thomas Youngs based on the time it would take for apples trees to reach maturity. He wrote in the *Youngs Record*:

> *For growing them under these conditions, it must be assumed that the seeds were planted, and some four years growth attained, before transplanting into a permanent orchard. After this, before any such production as the terms of the lease indicate, could be realized, from ten to fifteen years must have elapsed, even with favorable conditions. It is assumed, that this statement offers a reasonable conclusion, from the smallest figures given in it, that he must have been here eighteen years before 1670, the date of the lease.... From the above assumptions, which are nearly the equivalent of facts, he must have come to Oyster Bay Cove as soon as 1652, and it is not improbable as early as 1650. Either of the dates, if correct, proves that he was the first who settled at Oyster Bay Cove, and that he was established*

> *there, before any attempt was made for the settlement of Oyster Bay Village or any part of the Town of Oyster Bay, and that he was the pioneer of civilization in this part of Long Island.*

Daniel's method of dating the apple trees' growth to maturity appears to be fairly accurate. I checked this out with a distant cousin of mine, Peter Hayward, who is a third-generation operator of an extensive apple orchard in New Hartford, Connecticut. Peter confirmed the time frame but said it might be a little on the high side; a closer time frame would be around fourteen or fifteen years.

Daniel had first written about the 1670 lease in 1882, when he wrote the agricultural section of Munsell's, but in that work, he made no such claims to the early arrival of Thomas Youngs. In Munsell's history, he wrote, "Prominent mention is made of apple trees and nurseries as early as 1669 and 1670. Several leases of land are found. The following, seventeen years after settlement, is perhaps the most suggestive." He then copied the entire 1670 lease agreement into his story for Munsell's.

The story of the dating of Thomas Youngs arrival has been used in numerous local history books and writings. In Francis Irvin's book *Oyster Bay: A Sketch*, published by the Oyster Bay Historical Society, the story was described in considerable detail along with the added notation that the 1670 lease, upon which the dating story is based, survives in the Oyster Bay Town Records. This appears to have been an assumption on the part of the authors of *Oyster Bay, a Sketch*. A diligent search of all eight volumes of the printed Oyster Bay Town Records revealed no reference to the 1670 lease. The lease was probably among the Youngs family's papers as leases, which were not usually recorded into the town records. It would be very interesting to examine the original 1670 lease to see if a mistake was made when the record was transcribed for entry into the town records. When examining documents from the seventeenth and eighteenth century, the handwriting is often very poor, the spelling is atrocious by today's standards and numbers are frequently difficult to determine; for example, the number "9" often can be confused with the number "7" because of certain curlicues that were commonly used. After examining related records, it is clear that Daniel Kelsey Youngs made a mistake when he read the date as 1670, because Thomas's son, Richard, who was not born until 1674, is mentioned in the lease. This should have raised a red flag for Daniel to look further, but, instead, he went on to make the claim that the Youngs family arrived in Oyster Bay as early as 1650 based solely upon a misread lease date. Another further red flag for Daniel should have been that Thomas Youngs Jr., born around 1670, and Richard Youngs, born 1674, both signed the supposed 1670 lease agreement.

Thomas Youngs had first married Rebecca Mapes, who gave birth to two sons, John, born in 1668, and Thomas, born in 1670. Rebecca Mapes Youngs died sometime shortly thereafter, and Thomas Youngs was remarried to Elizabeth Harcurt, daughter of Richard Harcurt of Oyster Bay. Five children were born to Thomas and Elizabeth, including Richard, who was born around 1674 and is also mentioned in the lease. Thomas's eldest son, John Youngs, was married in 1690 to Ruth Elliot and settled in Stamford, Connecticut, on a grant his father had been given in 1673. The rest of the Youngs children remained in Oyster Bay. Thomas Youngs Sr. transferred ownership of his grant in Greenwich to his son John on December 2, 1689. In that record, he refers to himself as "once an inhabitant of Greenwich, Conn., now a resident of Oishter Bay, L. I." This statement gives support to the supposition that this Thomas Youngs, who was a witness to the sale of Black Tom, was the same Thomas Youngs who settled in Oyster Bay Cove.

In 1690, Thomas Jr. was about twenty years old and Richard was about sixteen; the rest of the children were all fourteen years old and younger. The dating of the lease at 1690 is in perfect timing with the marriage of the eldest son, John Youngs, who went to live in Connecticut, and with the coming of age of the next eldest two sons, Thomas Jr. and Richard. Thomas Youngs appears to have given Thomas Jr. and Richard the lease to operate the farm but wanted to ensure that the eldest son, John, had a share in the production of the farm, which accounts for the proviso for the barrels of apples reserved for John Youngs. The date of 1690 also ties in perfectly with the dating method used by Daniel Youngs based on the maturation of the apple trees. Thomas Youngs was granted land at Cove Neck in 1676, which allows fourteen years for the seeds to have grown and for the trees to have been transplanted and reach fruit bearing maturity before 1690.

Selah Youngs, author of the 1907 history of the Youngs family, had access to the lease and wrote, "Evidently it is a duplicate of the lease given to his sons, and the date, which, strange to say, is 1670, cannot be reconciled with the ages of his sons, as the son Richard was probably born about 1674. Hereafter something may be discovered to elucidate this apparent mystery." Perhaps, when this duplicate copy was made, an error was made when writing the date, but Selah Youngs offers no explanation other than the dates can't be reconciled. Daniel Youngs should have taken a closer look at the facts contained in other records before making his assumptions based on the 1670 date alone. From the records of the grant by the Town of Oyster Bay to Thomas Youngs on December 9, 1676, we can now determine, with some degree of reliability, that the earliest parts of the Youngs Homestead were built sometime in 1677.

In 1680, Thomas Youngs Sr.'s land holdings were increased when he was given a second town grant of six acres adjacent to his original three acres. In 1685, his father-in-law, Richard Harcurt, deeded to Thomas Youngs some of his lands in Cove Neck. Thomas Youngs began buying up the properties of his neighbors as they became available; by 1687, he had purchased the properties of Aaron Furman, Thomas Weekes and the remaining properties of his father-in-law, Richard Harcurt. Over the next several decades, his sons and descendants continued buying land in Cove Neck until the middle of the eighteenth century, when the Youngs family owned most of the land on the southern half of Cove Neck. One of the largest land purchases by the Young family took place in 1756, when Thomas's grandson Daniel Youngs (born in 1718) purchased fifty-nine acres from Benjamin Birdsall. Daniel and his brother, Thomas (born in 1716), later divided the family's properties. Thomas retained the old family homestead while Daniel took the "other house," as it was called in family papers, which was located on the north side of the Cove Road, opposite the family's cemetery. In some legal papers, the home was also referred to as the "Mansion House." Daniel Youngs was a weaver and learned the trade from Enoch Flower, to whom his father had indentured him on August 23, 1732, when Daniel was only fourteen years old. Upon the death of Daniel Youngs in 1784, Daniel Youngs Jr. (born in 1748) and his wife, Susanna, moved in with his father's brother, Thomas, who was the owner of the Youngs Homestead. Thomas Youngs was married to Mary Colwell, and they had no children before Mary died in 1785. Since Thomas Young had no heir, Daniel Young Jr. inherited the Youngs Homestead when his uncle died in 1797.

Captain Daniel Youngs's youngest son, Daniel Youngs III, inherited the homestead property from his father. Daniel was born in 1783 and married Maria Baker, daughter of John Baker, in 1815. They had eight children, including Daniel Kelsey Youngs, author of *The Youngs Record*. Daniel became a prosperous farmer and had a great interest in raising cattle. In 1822, his Durham cattle were awarded three silver cups and several silver spoons as premiums at the Queens County Fair. Daniel Youngs was elected a justice of the peace for the Town of Oyster Bay

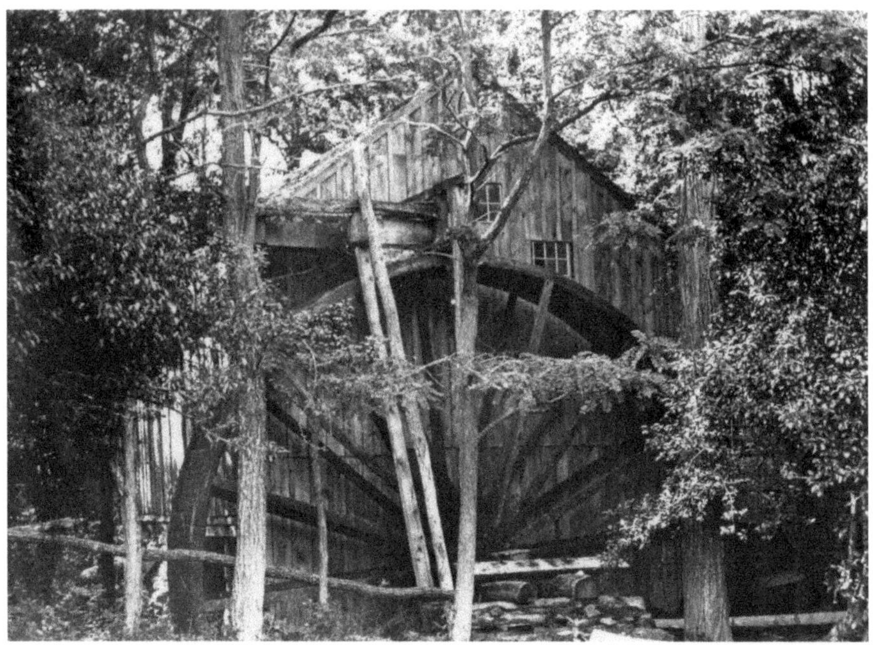

Arnold Fleet's Mill ground the grain of the early farmers of Cove Neck. *Courtesy John Hammond.*

and became known around the village as Squire Daniel Youngs. Daniel Youngs lived to be ninety years old before dying in 1874.

Daniel Kelsey Youngs inherited the Youngs Homestead upon the death of his father. He was born on May 7, 1817, and married Sarah Elizabeth, daughter of Daniel Smith and Frances Wortman, on October 10, 1850. His parents had intended for him to be schooled for a profession, but Daniel, although an excellent student at the Oyster Bay Academy, much preferred the outdoor life. He took over the management of his father's farm at the age of sixteen, and according to Selah Youngs, the farm became the "model farm of Long Island" under his care. Daniel was particularly interested in small fruits and market gardening, and he was an authority throughout the United States on the culture of asparagus. He was one of the founders, the first treasurer and a president of the Queens County Agricultural Society. In 1880, the Homestead Farm consisted of two hundred improved acres and one hundred acres of woodland. Livestock on the farm included fifty head of cattle, twelve swine and with three hundred chickens. Three hundred pounds of butter were made on the farm in 1879 and 1880, and the crops raised included 60 bushels of barley, 80 bushels of buckwheat, 600 bushels of Indian corn, 60 bushels of rye, 160 bushels of wheat and 600 bushels of potatoes. The apple orchard consisted of sixteen acres with five hundred fruit-bearing trees, which yielded 300 bushels of apples, valued at $150. It was that same year, 1880, when Daniel Kelsey Youngs sold land to James A. Roosevelt. The sale papers were not specific about exactly how much land was involved, but it described the parcel as "between sixty and seventy acres," which was valued at $250 per acre. A deposit of $500 was given to Daniel by Roosevelt on November 19, 1880, when he also signed an agreement that said:

> [The] *balance of said sum whenever the title to said premises shall have been ascertained—and the number of acres therein computed to the satisfaction of the said party of the second part. The examination of such title and the computation of such area to be consummated and ascertained with all reasonable dilligence* [sic].

Adjoining this parcel was the land of Thomas Youngs (born 1645). In 1883, Thomas Youngs sold 155 acres to Theodore Roosevelt. Roosevelt kept 95 of those acres, upon which he built *Sagamore Hill*, and sold the remainder to his uncle James A. Roosevelt.

5

GEORGE WASHINGTON AND THE YOUNGS FAMILY

Daniel Youngs, born on July 21, 1748, was the eldest son of Daniel Youngs and Hannah Underhill. He married Susanna Kelsey, who was born in 1752 to Timothy Kelsey and Keziah Ketchum of Huntington. He is referred to in various records and local histories as Captain Daniel Youngs. He had been captain of the local militia before the Revolutionary War and signed to support the Congress in 1776, but when the British took over Long Island following the Battle of Long Island in August 1776, Daniel Youngs, like many others who did not enlist into the Continental army or flee Long Island during its period of occupation (1776–1783), was compelled to take the oath of allegiance and submit to British military authority. After that, he became a captain in the local Tory militia. His unit consisted of himself as captain, Lieutenant George Weeks and Sergeants Justus Macoun, Daniel Weeks, Robert Wilson, Joseph Lattin and William Bennett. On his official return from March 20, 1781, Youngs listed one captain, one lieutenant, one ensign, four sergeants, four corporals and eighty privates, including twenty Quakers and a drummer. Militia units had the responsibility of gathering supplies for the British forces. Most of these collected supplies were brought to Youngs's dock to be loaded onto schooners for shipment to the British in New York. At the time, the dock was located in front of the Youngs Homestead, but it was later destroyed during a raid on Cove Neck in the winter of 1781.

As captain of the Oyster Bay unit, Daniel Youngs did far less than a commendable job. Some historians maintain that Captain Daniel Youngs was an active spy for George Washington; others state that he simply dragged out his foraging duties to impede the British demands for horses and firewood. Daniel Kelsey Youngs wrote that Captain Daniel Youngs "was a terror to the Hessian soldiers (who were stationed at Oyster Bay during the Revolution) after they tried to steal juice from his cider press." The Youngs family orchard was extensive at that time, as evidenced by the following passage from *Gaine's Mercury*, "December 18, 1768, the New York Society for Promoting Arts adjudged a premium of 10 Pounds to Thomas Youngs, of Oyster Bay, for the largest nursery of apple trees. It contains twenty-seven thousand one hundred and twenty-three trees." In March 1781, the record shows that Captain Daniel's unit had carted only fifty cords of the requisitioned six thousand cords of wood to the Oyster Bay landing. Major Kissam, an officer in the occupying British army, wrote to his commanding officer in Jamaica on March 18, 1782, that "a considerable part of the six thousand cords of wood remain yet due from the inhabitants, particularly about Oyster Bay."

Despite the fact that Daniel Youngs had been the captain of a Tory militia unit during the Revolutionary War, President George Washington selected the Youngs Homestead as one of his stopover points during his presidential tour of Long Island in April 1790. In his diary entry for Friday, April 23, 1790, George Washington recorded,

> *About 8 o'clock we left Roe's, and baited the horses at Smith's Town at a Widow Blidenberg's a decent house 10 miles from Setalkat—thence 15 miles to Huntington where we dined—and afterwards proceeded seven miles to Oyster Bay, to the House of a Mr. Young (private and very neat and decent) where we lodged.*

On the April 24, Washington recorded, "Left Mr. Youngs before 6 o'clock and passing Musqueto Cove breakfasted at a Mr. Underdunck's at the head of a little bay." Keziah Youngs, daughter of Captain Daniel Youngs, was married to Major William Jones and lived on the west shore of Cold Spring Harbor. Her father invited them over to the Youngs homestead on the evening of George Washington's visit. There is a family story in which it is said that President George Washington kissed Keziah on her cheek, and she vowed that no man would ever kiss her on that cheek again. It is obvious from George Washington's diary notes that he knew of Captain Daniel Youngs's service with the Tory militia. Mary Fanny Youngs wrote in her 1948 narrative, "[Washington] had his supper and stayed all night at the house of Captain Daniel Youngs, and we couldn't see why he stayed with a man who had been fighting against him." She goes on to relate how the family preserved the table where Washington dined along with the coffee pot and sugar bowl he used and the bed he slept in.

Many Youngs family members believed that Daniel Youngs had been a double agent during the Revolutionary War, which was the reason for George Washington's stay at the Youngs homestead in 1790. There were other intelligence agents at work in Oyster Bay during the Revolutionary War, including Robert Townsend, who was identified as being Culper Junior, an alias. According to Morton Pennypacker, the author of *Two Spies* and *George Washington's Spies*, when Sally Townsend of Raynham Hall needed to get a note to her brother Robert, she called upon Daniel Youngs for help. Youngs was sent for and asked to supply a messenger to take the note into New York City, where Robert was located. Another spy in Oyster Bay was William Roe, who furnished secret intelligence to the American cause in fall 1777; he was later betrayed by an informant, which led him to flee Oyster Bay to escape British vengeance.

After the war, Daniel Youngs was paid £200 by the American government on April 1, 1783, and again on July 16, 1783, for his services during the war. In all, Daniel Youngs was reimbursed over £1,000 for his personal expenditures during the war; rather unusual for a Tory militia captain. In 1893, William Jones Youngs presented a gift to the Matinecock Lodge of Freemasons in Oyster Bay. The gift was described by the secretary of the lodge as "an old relic, a charm worn by Brother ________." The secretary made no mention of the name of the wearer of the charm. Over the years, the charm was misplaced, so we are left to wonder if it was a masonic charm worn by George Washington that he left with the Youngs family as a memento of his 1790 visit.

6
WILLIAM JONES YOUNGS

In Theodore Roosevelt's own words, William Jones Youngs was the "keeper of [his] conscience." Few individuals or families had a greater impact on Roosevelt's political development than William Jones Youngs and the Youngs family of Oyster Bay. William Jones Youngs was born on June 24, 1851, in his maternal grandfather's house on Centre Island. He was the only child of Daniel Kelsey Youngs and Sarah Elizabeth Smith and was baptized at Christ Church in Oyster Bay on October 23, 1851. His mother was a daughter of Daniel Smith, Esq., a seventh-generation descendant of Captain John Underhill and a sixth-generation descendant of Major Thomas Jones and his wife, Freelove Townsend. His middle name, Jones, had been given to many others in the family to honor the memory of Major Thomas Jones.

Thomas Youngs came to Oyster Bay in the 1600s and made several purchases of land directly from the Matinecock Indians that were supplemented by several grants of land from the town freeholders. By the time of the Revolutionary War, the Youngs family property stretched a considerable distance north of the family homestead onto Cove Neck and included the 150 acres purchased by Theodore Roosevelt from the Youngs family on which Roosevelt built *Sagamore Hill.*

Daniel Kelsey Youngs, father of William Jones Youngs, was born in 1817 at the family homestead. He received his early education at the Oyster Bay Academy under the tutelage of Reverend Marmaduke Earle. Although his parents had wished for him to be educated for a profession Daniel Kelsey

Youngs preferred an agricultural life and undertook the management of his father's farm at age sixteen. Nevertheless, he became very well educated by extensive reading and research into the history of the Youngs family and the history of Long Island. Daniel Kelsey Youngs was one of the founders of the Queens County Agricultural Society. In 1890, he completed and published the *Oyster Bay Youngs Record,* a history and genealogy of the descendants of Thomas Youngs of Oyster Bay.

Growing up in the Youngs Homestead, one couldn't help but develop an interest in local history. The homestead had been built by the early settler Thomas Youngs in the 1600s and was passed on through many generations and ultimately to William Jones Youngs, the last of the line to own the homestead. During the period of the Revolutionary War, Captain Daniel Youngs lived in the homestead, which was owned at the time by his uncle Thomas Youngs.

William Jones Youngs was raised in the family homestead that was originally built by Thomas Youngs in the 1600s and received his early education in the local schools. His daughter, Mary Fanny Youngs, wrote in 1948 that her father had attended Huntington Union School and graduated in 1868. That same year, he became a member of the first freshman class at the new Cornell University in Ithaca, New York. While there, he became a member of the Chi Phi fraternity. (Reverend George Roe Van De Water, the first rector of Christ Church in Oyster Bay, was also a member of Chi Phi.) He graduated from Cornell in 1872 and began working at the law office of Benjamin W. Downing. On September 1, 1873, he was admitted to the New York Bar in the Supreme Court of the Second Judicial Department. William Jones Youngs quickly developed an interest in politics and became a delegate to the State Convention in 1876. In 1879, he was elected assemblyman for the First District of Queens County.

In 1879, William Jones Youngs married Eleanor Smith Youngs, a third cousin, who was the daughter of David Jones Youngs and Cornelia Townsend. She was born in Oyster Bay Cove on December 24, 1854. Their only child, Mary Fanny Youngs, was born on February 14, 1880. Eleanor Smith Youngs died on December 31, 1883, at age twenty-nine after a battle with Bright's disease of the kidneys. She was buried in the Youngs family cemetery, directly across Cove Road from the homestead. In 1886, William Jones Youngs was remarried to Helen Louise Mason. They had one child, Helen, who was born on April 20, 1887. William Youngs was widowed a second time when Helen Louise Youngs died on March 30, 1889, in childbirth. The unnamed son also died on the same day. Youngs was married a third time, in August

1891, to May Benson Emery of Mineola, New York. May Benson Emery Youngs and William Jones Youngs had a son named Daniel K. Youngs Jr., who was born in August 1894, but he only survived until October 1894.

In 1948, Mary Fanny Youngs dictated a narrative about the Youngs family for her young nieces; the following information about her father, William Jones Youngs, is quoted from that narrative:

> *He was one of the dearest and kindest men that ever lived, honest, fair to everyone, and generous, but never a very good businessman, nor one to make much money, and when he did have money, he was generous and careless with it, so that, as the saying is, it ran through his fingers, and it was your dear Great-Granny who saved and took care of it for him. He loved politics, however, and was clever at them, that is, he was interested in good government, and knew how to get on with all sorts of people, so that he could influence them to do what he thought was right. He worked as a defense lawyer for a while, but when I was about sixteen he was elected* [in 1896] *to be what is called the District Attorney of Queens County, which at that time took in all of what is now Nassau County, on Long Island.… But then the County was divided, and just at that time Theodore Roosevelt wanted to be elected Governor of New York. He knew that Father knew people all over the State, and was very friendly with them, so he asked him to go with him on a trip, all around the State, to arrange for meetings where the Colonel was to speak, see that he saw the right people, and manage all the details of the trip, which was made on a special train. There were a number of newspaper reporters on the train, and Father saw that they were all so comfortable, that when the trip was over, they wrote him a letter, and all signed their names to it, and Colonel Roosevelt signed it, too.*

Although there was wide acclaim for the work done by William Youngs in the campaign to elect Theodore Roosevelt, the praise was not universal. In Oyster Bay, William Youngs was chastised by the editor of the *East Norwich Enterprise* for neglecting the local Republican Party in its efforts to get a Wallace win over Congressman Townsend Scudder of Glen Head. The editor wrote in the November 5, 1898, edition:

> *William J. Youngs will never live long enough to explain satisfactorily to the Republican Party of this village how it is that he has failed to do anything for his party in his own home. It is common talk that he wishes Wallace beaten. I do not believe this but the vote here will show. Townsend*

Scudder will poll a very large vote. It is believed he is a sound money man and as his opponent is not known, the republicans will vote for him. There are many Masons here.

Mary Fanny's reference to the Masons alludes to Scudder's strong ties to the fraternity and William Jones Youngs's membership of Matinecock Lodge No. 806 in Oyster Bay. Townsend Scudder was a Democrat and William Jones Youngs was a very active Republican, but perhaps the fraternal ties between the two were stronger than their political differences. Youngs and Scudder were also both working together on the formation of Nassau County, which was on the ballot that year. Congressman Townsend Scudder was reelected by a large margin.

Mary Fanny continued:

Well, the outcome of all this was that the Colonel was elected Governor, and he was so pleased with all that Father had done, that he asked him to come to Albany with him, and be Secretary to the Governor—be with him in his office, attend to his letters, see people for him, and make sure that he saw everyone he ought to see, and that he didn't see people who shouldn't have bothered him, and generally keep him in touch with what he should know, and free from what he shouldn't be troubled with.

Mary Fanny's assessment of her father's importance to Roosevelt was affirmed by Roosevelt in a letter he wrote to May Emery Youngs, Mary Fanny's stepmother, on August 28, 1899. William Jones Youngs had become ill with typhoid fever and was unable to carry out his regular duties in Albany. Roosevelt knew about typhoid fever, since it was the cause of the death of his own mother fifteen years earlier, and he was very concerned with Youngs's condition. William Loeb, who was then a stenographer to the state assembly, came to Roosevelt's office to fill in during Youngs's illness. From that time on, Loeb was steadily promoted. He eventually became Roosevelt's highly valued, confidential secretary during the presidency. Roosevelt wrote the following to May Youngs:

How is Mr. Youngs? I hope he is getting along all right. Since learning that the fever was broken, we have felt comparatively at ease. There is only one thing I should like to get an expression of opinion from him about when he is strong enough. I should like to increase Mr. Loeb's salary from $1,200 to $1,800 a year. This summer he has acted as my private secretary here at

> *Oyster Bay and has done invaluable work, showing excellent judgment as well as the utmost alertness and industry. Even when I am at Albany his work is not as mechanical as that of the other stenographers. As you know, I have made Mr. Youngs very much the keeper of my conscience, especially in all matters connected with the office, and I do not like to take any step of this kind without consulting him. But I do not want him consulted until he is well enough not to mind it. Faithfully Yours, Theodore Roosevelt.*

While ill, Youngs convalesced at the Chi Psi Lodge, his old Cornell University fraternity house. He lingered with a high fever for weeks and did not show significant improvement until the first week in September. At that time, he was allowed to go outside briefly and locate a telephone to call Albany. By the following week, he reported he was still feeling weak but that he and Mrs. Youngs had left Ithaca and returned to Albany on Superintendent Van Etten's, superintendent of the New York Central Railroad, personal railcar. On September 11, 1899, Billy Youngs was at his desk in Albany for the first time since July 18. When interviewed about his illness, he said, "I guess I managed to convalesce pretty fast. My physician seemed to think I had a tough constitution, but then I ought to have, for I hadn't been ill before since I was ten years old." The *Oyster Bay Guardian*

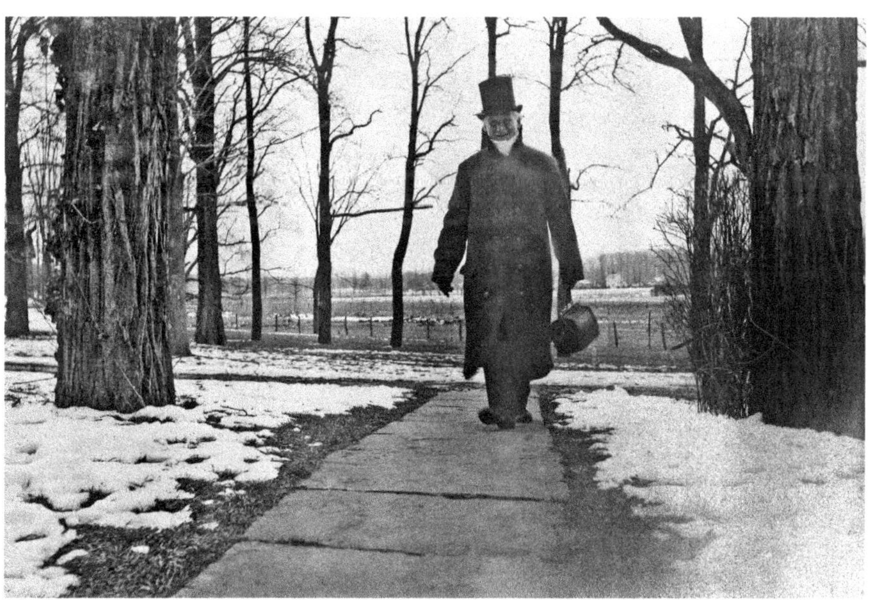

Dr. Peter Frye tended to the medical needs of many of the residents of Cove Neck. *Courtesy of the Oyster Bay Historical Society.*

reported that Youngs had returned to Oyster Bay briefly during the week of September 29, 1899, and was looking extremely well, but his voice was very husky, and he was unable to speak aloud.

Youngs did, however, have further health problems while in Albany. He was laid low in his room at the Ten Eyck Hotel in Albany in May 1900 as he entered the room with State Attorney General Davies. The *Brooklyn Eagle* reported that he was struck by a piece of falling stucco, but the *Oyster Bay Guardian* claimed it was a heavy piece of woodwork. Whichever it was, it made a severe gash in Youngs's forehead; Attorney General Davies immediately came to his aid, and several stitches were required to close the wound. Although badly bruised, he still reported to his office in the executive chamber. He was, again, struck with a debilitating fever in September 1900, which forced him to abandon Roosevelt's campaign trip to the West. William Youngs returned to Oyster Bay to recover. Fortunately, it was just a severe cold and not a return of the dreaded typhoid fever.

Continuing with Mary Fanny's narrative:

> *We were in Albany for two years, while the Colonel was Governor, and then, much against his will, he was made Vice-President of the United States, when William McKinley was elected president in 1900. He could not take Father to Washington as his secretary, because the Vice-President didn't have a secretary, only a stenographer to type his letters, and for a little while we were worried again, because Father had given up his law business to go with the Colonel, and it was very hard to get started again. But one day, a crazy man shot and killed poor President McKinley, and all of a sudden, Theodore Roosevelt was President! And then he remembered what a good district attorney Father had been, and asked him if he would like to be the United States attorney for the eastern district of New York, which meant that he would prosecute persons who broke United States laws, just as he had the ones who broke New York State laws—and of course Father said yes, he would, so the President appointed him for four years, then in four years, appointed him again, and then in four more years, Mr. Taft had been elected, and Father had been such a good attorney, that he appointed him for still another term, so he held that office for twelve years....I have told you how good he was; he could also be very serious, dignified and wise, but he was also very funny, and also he did most unexpected things, so that one never knew quite what he would do next. When there was anything important to be done he was serious about it, but at home he kept us guessing, quite often. He was*

quick-tempered, and would get very mad at us, and scold like anything, and in five minutes, he would be all over it, and have his arm around us. He had a lot of the funniest little tricks; he used to have bad headaches, and he said that when he had them as a boy, he wrapped his head up in one of his mother's flannel petticoats, and nothing but a flannel petticoat was good for his headaches, and he somehow got hold of one, and kept it, and as long as he lived, he wrapped his head up in that old petticoat, when it ached! He had a perfectly nice dressing-gown, but Mother bought him a lovely new silk quilt, lined with wool, crimson on one side and with lovely pink and crimson flowers on the other, and for the rest of his life, instead of wearing his dressing gown he would wrap himself up in that quilt, like an Indian in a blanket, with one corner of it trailing behind him like a tail, and parade all over the house in that costume!

But he had more friends, and more people loved him than happens to most men. Old and young, rich and poor, high and low, they came to his funeral and wrote us the most wonderful letters, when he died, and while he was never rich, and was not a great man, I want you to remember that he was loved and honored because he was honorable, wise and, above all, fair and kind.

To illustrate her father's sense of humor, Mary Fanny Youngs wrote the following anecdote about Christmas at the Cove School:

One Christmas, however, we had a funny time at the Cove School Christmas tree. It was when the Colonel was Governor of New York, and Father was his secretary, and because of having the Governor at the Christmas tree, there were several reporters there, from the New York papers. Mr. Washburn and Mr. Russell were there, and an old gentleman with long side whiskers, Dr. Cooley, the County School Commissioner. Mr. Washburn made a long, dry speech, and Mr. Russell made a long prayer, and Dr. Cooley made a longer and worse speech than Mr. Washburn, and the Governor made a shorter and nicer speech, but by that time everyone was nearly dead, and when Miss Provost called on Father to make a speech, we all expected another long talk, we hoped not too bad. But Father was also tired of long, dry speeches, so up he got, and said "Now, the Governor, and these other gentlemen have made beautiful talks and prayers, but I have heard you little boys and girls speak your pieces, and I have been thinking that I would like to speak my piece." With that he made a little bow, and launched forth into "Jimmy Sliderlegs,"

> *which your mother must read to you. He acted just like a bashful little boy, and made funny gestures, and Helen heard a reporter say "Who is that guy?"—at first, every one stared at him as if he were crazy, and then Mrs. Roosevelt began to laugh, and the Governor shouted, and by that time all the children were laughing. When Father came to the end—"All that was left, was a lock of his hair," he grabbed a lock of his own hair, stood it up on his forehead like a horn, made another bow, and sat down, with everybody laughing and clapping and stamping, and the Colonel and Mrs. Roosevelt never forgot it, but thirty years afterwards, Mrs. Roosevelt sent me an old copy of "Jimmy Sliderlegs," to remember it by.*

Mary Fanny Youngs died on April 17, 1960, and she was also buried at Youngs Memorial Cemetery.

After being elected as Queens County district attorney, Judge Youngs rented out the Homestead at Cove Neck and moved to 26 Cathedral Avenue, Garden City, New York, in order to be closer to his work. Youngs continued to serve in this position through the administrations of President Taft and President Wilson. He died on April 27, 1916, in Garden City and was buried in Youngs Memorial Cemetery. Following the death of her husband, May Youngs began selling off what remained of the Youngs family property. In 1929, May sold the Youngs Homestead to Stuart L. Craig, who later sold the property to Philip James (PJ) Roosevelt Jr. in 1952. PJ had a wonderful sense of humor, and he often told the story of how the Youngs, who were English, planted an English elm tree back in the 1600s that had grown over the centuries until it was recognized as the largest of its variety in the United States. In reference to his Dutch ancestors, he said that shortly after he bought the property in 1952, the English elm tree died from the Dutch Elm disease. Although, for many generations, all the Manhattan-bred Roosevelts had been buried in Greenwood Cemetery in Brooklyn, Theodore Roosevelt chose the family cemetery of the Youngs family in Oyster Bay as his final resting place.

On the evening before his death, Theodore Roosevelt felt uncomfortable, and his family members called their neighbor, Dr. George Washington Faller. Dr. Faller gave Roosevelt something to calm him and to ease some of his pain. Upon retiring for the night, Roosevelt spoke his final words to his trusted valet, James Amos: "James, would you please put out the light, I want to go to sleep." Dr. George Faller recorded on Roosevelt's death certificate that the former president expired at 4:15 a.m. on January 6, 1919. He listed the cause of death as an "embolism of the lung." On the afternoon of his

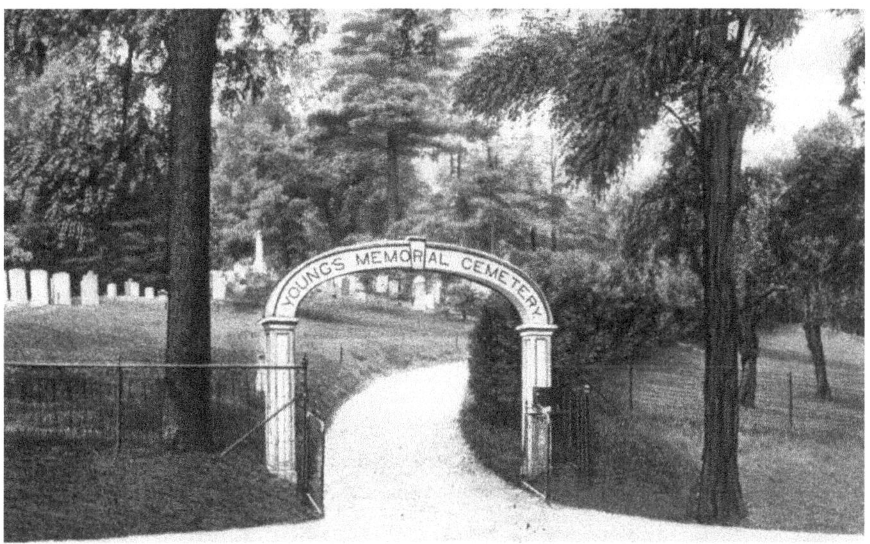

The entrance to Youngs Memorial Cemetery, where Theodore Roosevelt, William Jones Youngs, Reverend George Roe VanDeWater, Henry Dollard and so many other residents of Cove Neck are buried. *Courtesy John Hammond.*

death, three airplanes of his late son Quentin's unit flew over *Sagamore Hill* and dropped wreaths of laurel close by the large elm tree.

Before their deaths, William Youngs sold a plot in the Youngs family cemetery, where Youngs family members had been buried since the 1600s along with their slaves, to Roosevelt. Funeral arrangements were made by Wilbur Johnson, the local undertaker in East Norwich. Roosevelt had planned everything out long before his death. At noon, on January 8, 1919, the family and several close friends assembled in the trophy room of *Sagamore Hill* for a short funeral service. Earlier, Roosevelt's close friend social reformer Jacob Riis sat Shivas. Roosevelt's widow, Edith, stayed at *Sagamore Hill* reading the printed funeral service while their family and friends went down to Christ Church in Oyster Bay. The hearse carrying Roosevelt was escorted by a large contingent of uniformed New York City policemen on horseback.

Roosevelt's funeral service was one of the simplest, in terms of ceremony, that anyone could recall for a man of such prominence. There were no honorary pallbearers, no distinguished ushers and no music was played during the service. Although, Reverend George Talmage did read the words to Roosevelt's favorite hymn "How Firm a Foundation." About five hundred persons were present for the service and there were hundreds of

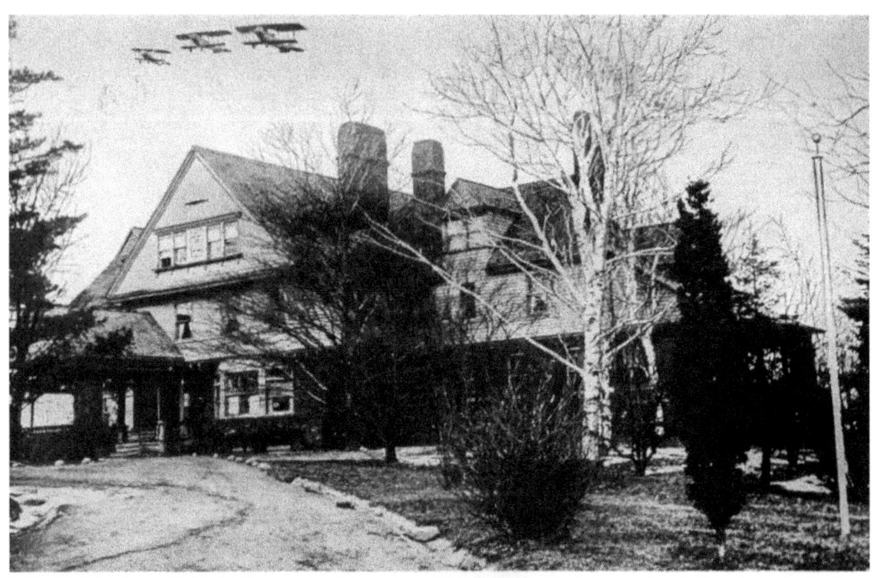

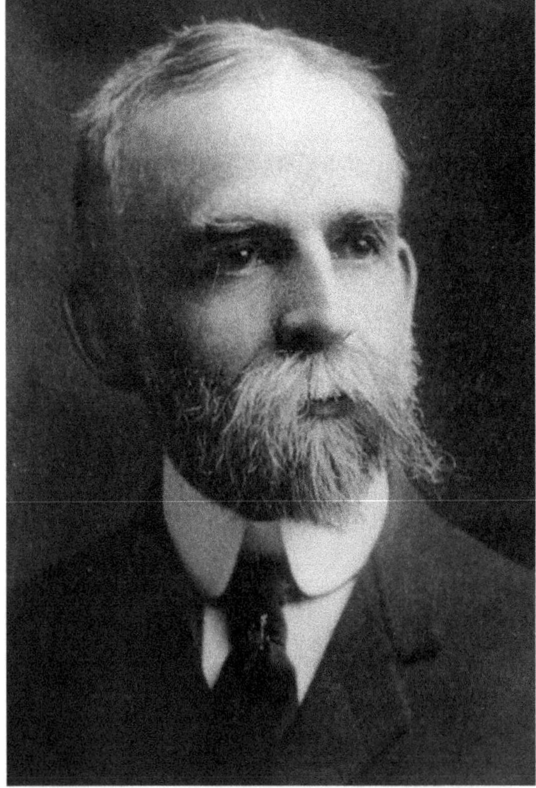

Above: Three airplanes from Quentin Roosevelt's unit flew over *Sagamore Hill* on the afternoon of Theodore Roosevelt's death. *Courtesy of Sagamore Hill National Historic Site.*

Left: Dr. George Washington Faller was called by the family when Theodore Roosevelt took ill on the evening of January 5, 1919. Roosevelt died during the night. *Courtesy John Hammond.*

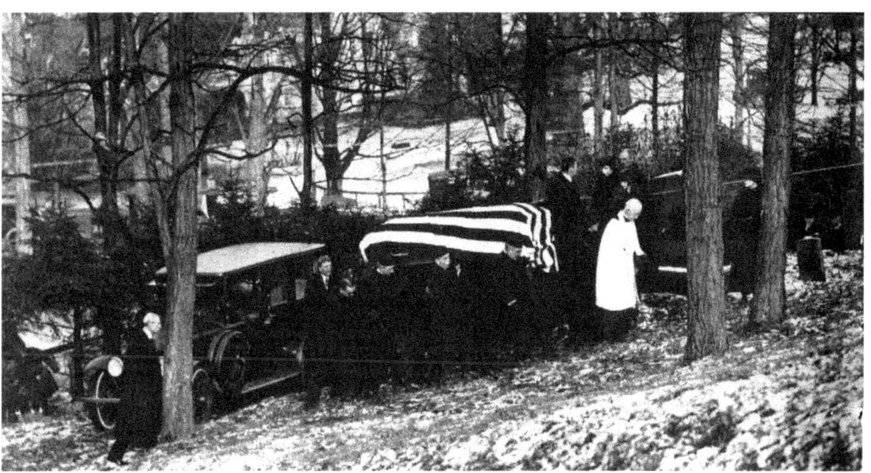

Theodore Roosevelt's coffin is carried up the hill at Youngs Memorial Cemetery. Reverend Alexander Gatherer Russell leads the procession. *Courtesy of Sagamore Hill National Historical Site.*

local residents sitting on the snowy hill by the Presbyterian church, where Roosevelt had attended church as a youth and where his father had been an elder. East Main Street, leading up to Youngs Cemetery, was lined with residents and schoolchildren for its entire length as the funeral cortege made its way. There was another brief ceremony at the graveside; among the mourners was former president William Howard Taft, who had lost his bid for reelection in 1912 when Roosevelt came in second as a third-party candidate. It was reported that Taft was among the very last to leave; he stood on the snowy hillside with his head bowed, sobbing profusely.

7
YOUNGS STORE AND CHAPEL

The Youngs family properties included much more than farms and the homestead, such as a store that was operated by David J. Youngs. David lived in the "Over the Brook House," which later became the Storrs residence. The Brook House, as it was also called, was built around 1800, according to Mary Fanny Youngs. She also wrote, "Next to the Chapel, on the Huntington Road, was the Other House." Shortly after the death of David J. Youngs, in 1881, the Brook House was purchased by William Jones Youngs, who was also a partial owner of the Youngs Homestead at the time. There is no record telling us when the store was built, but we do know that it was located on the lot on the corner of Cove Road and Cove Neck Road, next to the "Other House." The store was a second location of Jones and Youngs, a general store in Oyster Bay village. The Jones and Youngs village store was located on the west side of South Street in the space that became Audrey Avenue around 1889. The store in Cove Neck was converted to a chapel in 1878, according to a brief article in the *Long Islander* from November 22, 1878, that said, "The Episcopalians are altering the old store on Mr. Youngs's property for the purpose of converting it to a Chapel."

Mary Fanny Youngs wrote a little about the family store in her narrative:

> *Across* [Cove Neck Road] *from the Homestead was a building which once had been a store, but it had been made into a dwelling house at one end, and the other end was made into a plain little chapel, where we had Sunday School, and sometimes the minister came from Oyster Bay village*

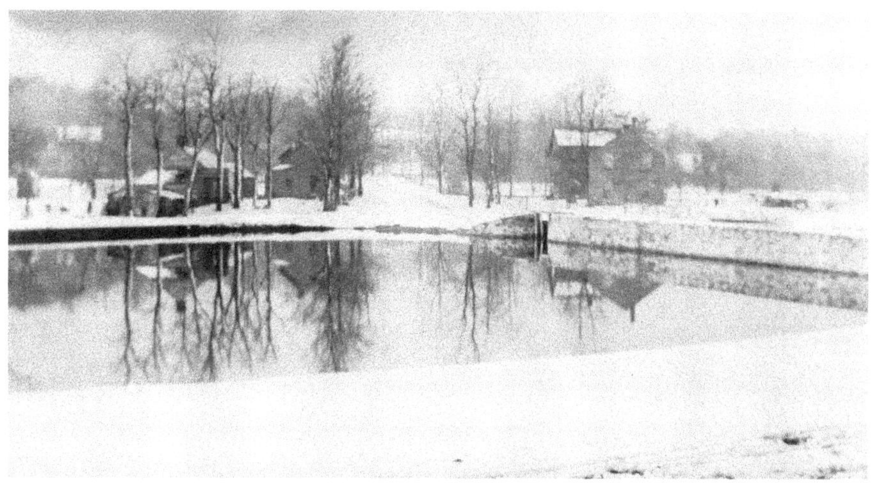

The pond in front of the Brook House on Cove Neck Road, where Billy Youngs lived in the 1800s. All of the buildings were owned by Youngs family members. *Courtesy of Raynham Hall Museum.*

> *for services. I am sure that Uncle Tom and Grandpa and some of the neighbors fitted that little chapel up themselves. I know that either Uncle Tom or Grandpa David made the lovely wooden cross on the altar, and that the two white vases, and the bronze candlesticks were from the Homestead. This building was pulled down, later and the candlesticks are on the library mantel here in Garden City, and every time I look at them, I think of that little bare chapel, and the dear good old minister, Mr. Washburn, and the good people who used to go there when I was a little girl.*

Francis Irvin wrote in her 1950 book *Oyster Bay: A Sketch*, "The old Cove Chapel stood where the Arboretum now stands. Once a month, early Communion and evening services were held there, and, at times, the Cove's weddings, christenings and funerals took place. The Cove Schoolhouse looked down from higher ground." The arboretum property was part of the parcel sold by May Emery Youngs to Samuel Reading Bertron on September 10, 1927. After Bertron's death, his heirs sold the arboretum property to the Village of Cove Neck on December 6, 1938.

After the building was partially converted into a tenement, the old store was occupied by David and Catherine Garvin, who both worked for the Youngs family at the homestead. Mary Fanny Youngs wrote about how she didn't care much for David Garvin, but she greatly admired Catherine Garvin, of whom she said:

> [She] *could do almost anything; cook, clean house, help with the pig-killing work, and when we used to send asparagus to market, as we sometimes did, several people would come to help bunch it, in holders that held just one bunch, then the bunches were tied up with raffia, or palm fibre, and packed in big wooden boxes with rope handles to send off to market, and Catherine could bunch faster than anybody else.*

The Youngs children all called the farm workers and household help by their first names, but Catherine Garvin would not allow it. Mary Fanny Youngs wrote, "She also informed me that I was not to call her Catherine until I was sixteen years old; when I was sixteen, I would be a young lady, and might call her Catherine, but until then, I was a little girl, and I was to treat her with respect, and call her Mrs. Garvin—which I did!"

David and Catherine were the parents of Mary Ann Garvin, who married Franklin Hall. Franklin Hall also worked for the Youngs but lived with his family in a separate house on the homestead grounds. Hall left the Youngs to work at *Sagamore Hill* for Theodore Roosevelt around 1896. Johnnie Garvin, brother of Mary Ann, was the coachman for the Youngs and took care of the horses. He lived with his parents until the early 1890s, when he took a job in Flushing as coachman for David Youngs. The old store building was disassembled in November 1900, and most of the material from the building was used to erect a new two-story structure on the opposite side of the road.

The grandpa referred to by Mary Fanny Youngs was David Jones Youngs, who was born on June 25, 1818, and died on May 4, 1881. He married Cornelia Townsend, daughter of Dr. James C. Townsend and Ann Valentine. David Jones Youngs was a son of Samuel Youngs, who lived at Elmwood for many years. David Jones Youngs and Cornelia Townsend had four children: Samuel, James, Eleanor Smith Jones (who married William Jones Youngs, the father of Mary Fanny Youngs) and Cornelia Townsend Youngs (who married Reverend George Roe Van De Water, rector of Christ Church in Oyster Bay). Elmwood was built in 1836 by Henry Youngs, brother of Thomas F. Youngs. *Elmwood* was later owned by Louis Comfort Tiffany for many years before he renamed the place the *Elms*.

David Jones Youngs, son of Samuel Youngs and his second wife, Phoebe Reynolds, inherited the family home, Over the Brook, and farm. However, in 1877, he ran into financial troubles and had to assign all of his property, including his farm and Jones and Youngs general store, to the benefit of creditors. The bulk of the farm was eventually purchased by David's cousin

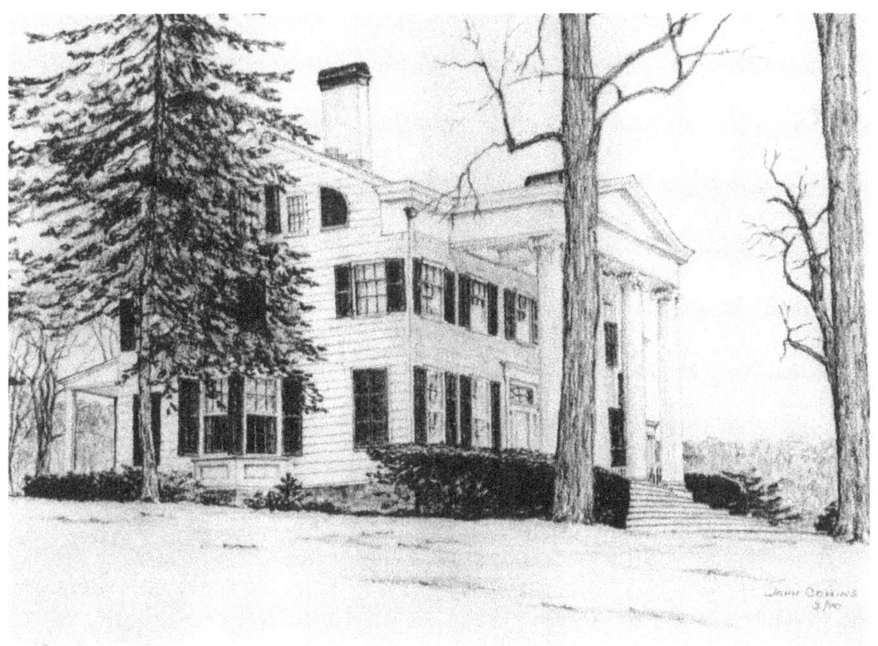

Elmwood was built in 1836 by Thomas Youngs and his brother. It was known as "The Tiffany Place" for many years. This drawing, by John Collins, originally appeared in the publication *Walls Have Tongues. Courtesy of the Oyster Bay Historical Society.*

of the next generation, William Jones Youngs. William was also the partial owner of the Youngs Homestead and other lands of Daniel Jones Youngs Esq. He was also the son-in-law of David J., having married his daughter Eleanor. The farm taken over by William Jones Youngs consisted of eighty-five acres of land.

8

THE YOUNGS SCHOOL AND ZACHARIAH WEEKES

In 1890, Daniel Kelsey Youngs wrote in the *Youngs Record* about his grandfather Thomas Youngs, who was born in 1717:

> *He built and owned the school house located on the top of Cove Hill, where all of the Cove children, and many from Oyster Bay Village, a mile at the west, attended school. This attendance, from the village, is believed to have been from necessity, as no record, or evidence of any kind is found, that a building for school purposes had ever been erected elsewhere, in or near the village. The use of this school house was gratuitously given for a public school, until the academy in the village was opened for instruction in 1801. Soon after that it was moved to the east side of the hill and converted into a tenement, where, with additions and renovations, it is still extant.*

The school was built on the Cove Hill in 1758. It was built to the west of the Youngs Homestead, and the first schoolmaster was Phebe Weeks.

Zachariah Weekes wrote in his diary, "Tuesday Febr. 21, 1758 Yesterday Morning Phebe Weeks Began to keep School in the Cove." The earliest mention of the school building is also from the diary of Zachariah Weekes, on February 19, 1758, when he wrote, "Carman and Joseph Townsend come there in their way as they went about to git a school up in the woods." On February 26, 1758, he wrote, "To Day Robert Colwell and Gill McCoun went about Town to try to git me a School in the Town Schoolhouse." Zachariah finally moved into the school on March 6, 1758, when he wrote in his diary, "Moved this Day by Mr. Colwell into the School House in Oyster

Bay." On March 13, 1758, Weekes wrote, "There is now a Confounded Rout about the School that I am in With French John and Just. Town. and my imployers....My imployers Met here to Conclude upon something With the French Man and Left it to Ju. McCoun to git Some Boards of Dan. Parish But he is so conscious that he will Not let him have them." The various difficulties were obviously worked out, as Zachariah continued working in the school until his death at age forty in 1771.

Zachariah Weekes was born on December 20, 1730, to Silas Weekes and Sarah Rogers. His father died the year before the school was built, on November 26, 1757. The Weekes family's homestead, on the corner of Sandy Hill Road and East Main Street, did not pass to Zachariah despite him being the only surviving son of Silas Weekes. Instead, the home was passed to his sister, Ann Weekes, who had married Richard Latting. The reason for this was probably that Zachariah was unmarried and also suffered from some kind of disability.

In addition to his diary, Zachariah also kept a ledger of the school's activities, which were almost entirely financial. He also recorded that between 1758 and 1771, the school had fifty pupils, whom he mentioned by their family names: Townsend, Underhill, McCoun, Weekes and Latting. His salary was rarely ever paid in hard money; some pupils paid him through service, like doing his laundry, knitting socks and making bread, and others brought him firewood, meat, hardware, shoes, et cetera. Tuition was seven shillings per quarter, and the equivalent value of the various goods was entered into Zachariah's ledger. Alice Delano Weekes, a distant cousin who lived in the nineteenth century and wrote about the family and Oyster Bay, wrote many years ago, "The accounts rarely balance in Zachariah's favor." Zachariah supplemented his school income by writing deeds and serving as a witness to various documents and transactions.

On May 1, 1768, Zachariah bought a twenty-four-year-old slave named Nab, or Abigail; her seven-year-old son, Jacob; and her two-year-old daughter, Hannah. Zachariah made no mention of the slaves in his diary, but we know from a copy of the purchase deed that he purchased them from Daniel McCoun, who also gave Zachariah a mortgage on the purchase. After his death, Zachariah was buried beside his mother and father in the family burial ground behind the Weekes family homestead on East Main Street. The schoolhouse was moved shortly after the opening of the Oyster Bay Academy, in 1801, and became the home of the Ryerson family. George Ryerson's unmarried daughters lived in the house well into the 1950s, when it was torn down, near collapse. It stood on the southeast lot of Baker Hollow Lane.

9
THE SWAN FAMILY

Oyster Bay attorney William Peck researched the history of many properties in Oyster Bay Cove and Cove Neck. His excellent research noted the following in regard to the Swan properties at Cove Neck:

> *Before his financial troubles, David J. Youngs (son of Samuel Youngs and his second wife, Phebe Reynolds) sold off a large portion of the farm. In 1853, he sold off 187 acres to Edward H. Swan and Benjamin L. Swan. Edward bought the southern 98 acres of this tract (later Merle-Smith), and Benjamin the northern 89 acres. Both built houses on their respective estates.*

Benjamin Lincoln Swan Jr. Property

Benjamin Lincoln Swan Jr. was born in New York City on July 7, 1818, and was the eldest son of Benjamin Lincoln Swan (June 15, 1787–January 23, 1866), a very wealthy New York merchant. Benjamin Swan was a member of the shipping firm Otis Dwight & Swan, which was based in Boston, and acted as its New York representative. In the early 1820s, the firm ceased operations and Swan subsequently became a very wealthy real estate investor. In the 1850 United States Census, he reported the value of his real estate at $350,000. His middle name, Lincoln, was used in the Swan family for

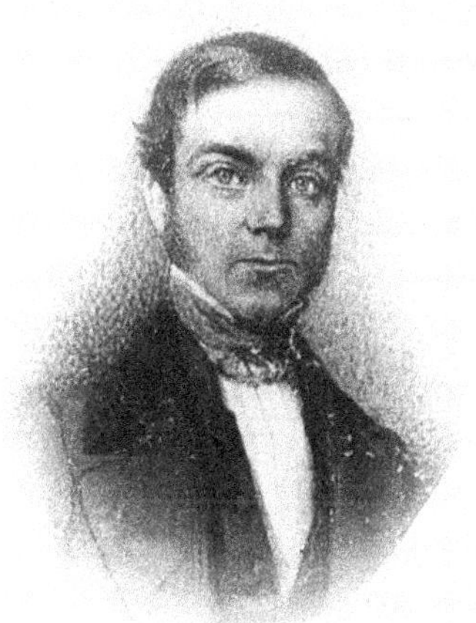

Left: Benjamin Lincoln Swan Jr. bought eighty-nine acres adjoining his brother's purchase of ninety-eight acres on Cove Neck from David J. Youngs in 1853. *Courtesy of the Oyster Bay Historical Society.*

Below: Benjamin Lincoln Swan Jr. built this home on Cove Neck shortly after purchasing the property. His son, William Lincoln Swan, inherited the property in 1902. *Courtesy of the Oyster Bay Historical Society.*

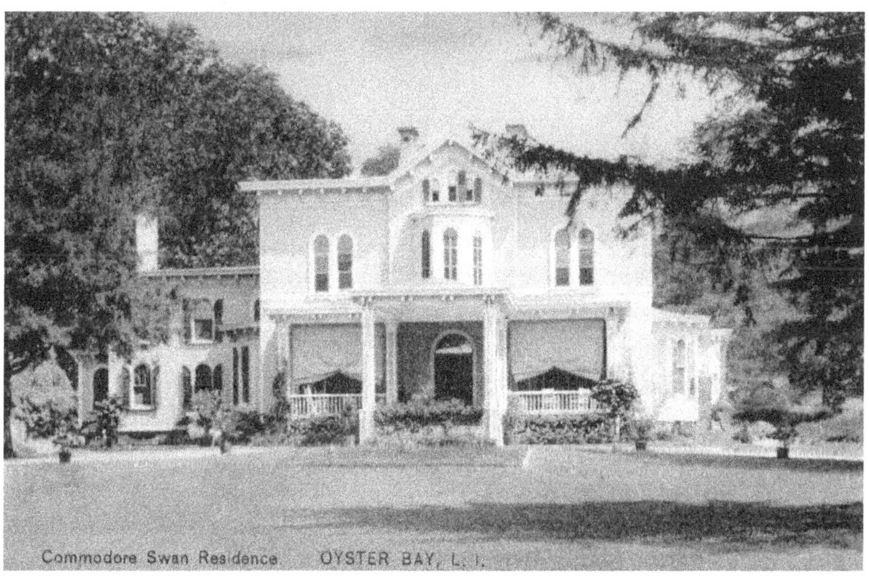

several generations to honor the memory of Samuel Swan II, who was an officer on the staff of General Benjamin Lincoln during Shays's Rebellion of 1786. General Benjamin Lincoln was also a hero of the American Revolutionary War; he had personally received the sword of surrender from British general Lord Cornwallis at Yorktown, Virginia. Samuel Swan greatly admired General Lincoln and named his firstborn son after him. This son was Benjamin Lincoln Swan, who was born 1787.

Benjamin Lincoln Swan Jr. graduated from Amherst College, married Caroline Post on October 16, 1844, and joined the Swan family investment

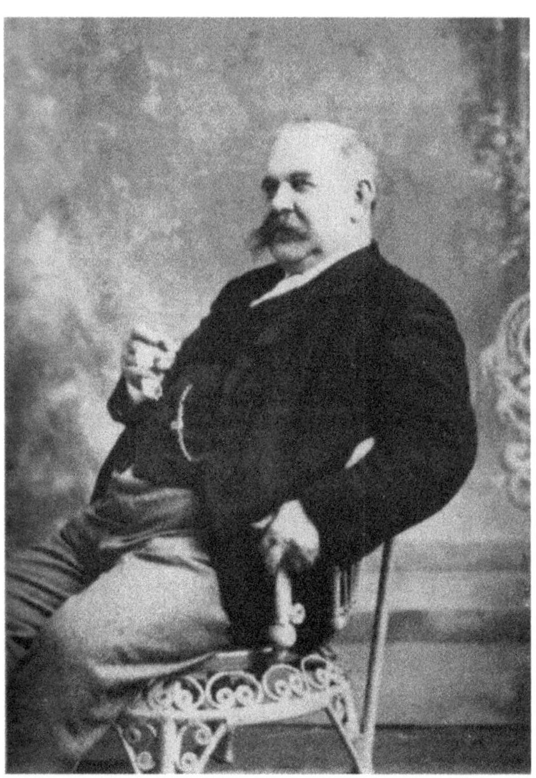

William Lincoln Swan moved into the home he inherited from his stepmother in 1902. In 1924, he moved to Baltimore to live with his daughter. *Courtesy John Hammond.*

business. He was also a member of the Union League Club and the New York and Century Clubs. Edward Henry Swan was born on March 14, 1822, also in New York City. He attended Harvard and Columbia Universities and married Julia S. Post on April 11, 1849. She was the younger sister of his brother, Benjamin's, wife, Caroline Post. In 1853, the two Swan brothers bought a large portion of the Youngs family holdings on Cove Neck from David J. Youngs. The purchases involved two adjoining parcels totaling 187 acres, with Benjamin buying the northern 89 acres for $8,443 and Edward buying the remaining 98 acres for $9,331. Both properties ran across Cove Neck from Oyster Bay Harbor to Cold Spring Harbor. The 1860 United States Census agricultural section listed Benjamin Swan's property at 87 acres. He reported owning eleven horses, three milk cows, six other cattle and three bovine (sheep), which he valued at $2,000. The 1867 Oyster Bay tax book lists Edward H. Swan's property consisting of 95 acres valued at $10,000 and Benjamin L. Swan's property consisting of 90 acres valued at $10,000.

Edward Swan Property

Edward Swan hired the noted New York architect John W. Ritch to design his home. A contract was signed on July 23, 1855, that said the home was to be completed by the builder, Osborn & Fish, by July 1, 1856. On the evening of Sunday, November 14, 1858, Edward Swan was retiring for the night when he noticed flames shooting past his bedroom window at the rear of the house. The rear piazza and stoop were on fire. The household staff had been given the weekend off, so Swan quickly gathered his family and they rapidly exited from the house. A stiff breeze had caused the fire to rapidly spread, engulfing the entire house. The house was easily visible from the village, where the alarm was sounded in the form of the ringing of the church bell. Village residents responded quickly, but there was little they could do other than stand and watch the conflagration. The intensity of the fire was exacerbated by the large amount of coal that had been brought in for the winter season. News of the fire reached all the way to New Orleans, where the November 26, 1858 *Times-Picayune* reported, "On the evening of the 14th inst. the splendid mansion of Edward Swann, Esq., at Oyster Bay, Long Island, was destroyed by fire. Its cost was $40,000. The furniture, which was also destroyed, was worth $10,000."

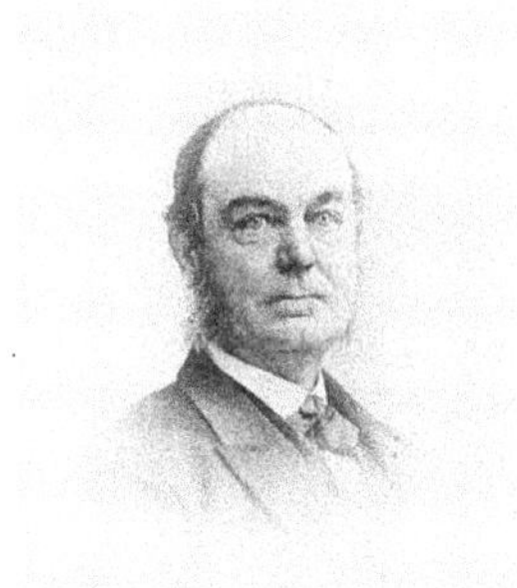

Edward H. Swan bought the southernmost ninety-eight acres adjoining his brother Benjamin's purchase of eighty-nine acres on Cove Neck from David J. Youngs in 1853. Edward's first home was completed in 1856, but, in 1858, it was destroyed by fire. *Courtesy of the Oyster Bay Historical Society.*

Edward Swan did not rebuild immediately. According to family stories, the fire that destroyed the Edward Swan house in 1858 so disturbed Edward's wealthy father, Benjamin Swan, that he financed the design and rebuild for his son. They hired the same architect, John W. Ritch, to design a new house for him. Ritch was both an engineer and an architect, and his designs included banks and hospitals as well as houses. The new house contract was signed on February 2, 1871, and the construction was set to cost $27,491. Plans called for the home's completion by June 1, 1871. The new house became known as the *Evergreens* and was built in the French Second Empire style. Robert MacKay described it, saying, "[It is a house] built in masonry with a slate roof and cast-iron porches. With its tripartite façade with a projecting central pavilion, round-headed windows, and mansard

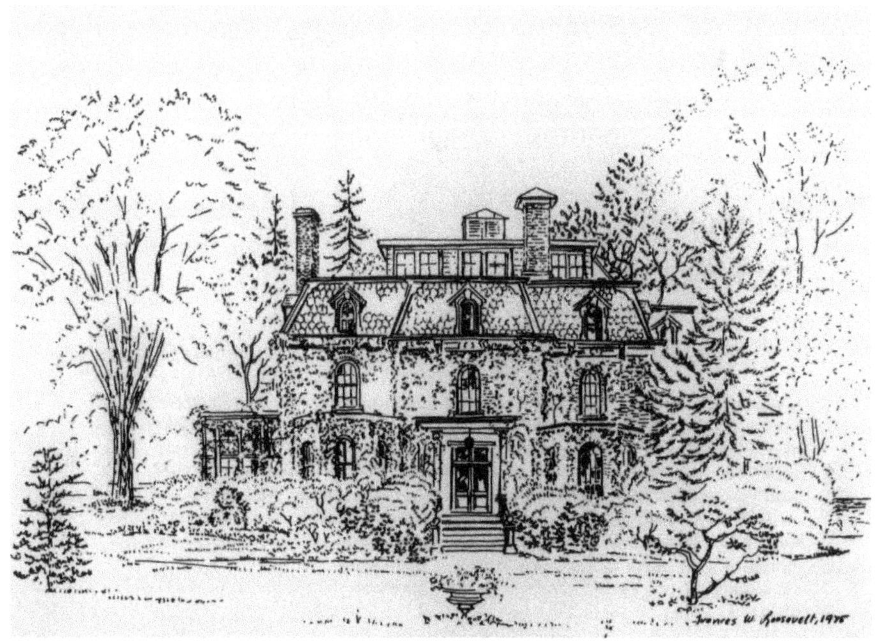

The Swan-Mathers house served as the village hall during the term of Mayor William H. Mathers. This was the 1871 rebuilt home of Edward H. Swan, which was sold to VanSantvoord Merle-Smith in 1919. This drawing was done by Frances Roosevelt in 1975. *Courtesy of the Oyster Bay Historical Society.*

roof, Edward's residence quickly became one of the early showplaces of Oyster Bay's summer colony." Edward Swan used his home at Cove Neck as his primary residence, where he greatly enjoyed growing roses. He devoted over seventy-five acres of his property to growing roses that he would ship in large quantities to hospitals throughout New York City. His brother, Benjamin, spent most of his time at his 5 West Seventieth Street, New York City residence and used his Cove Neck home as a summer residence.

The Swan brothers were members of the Fifth Avenue Presbyterian Church in New York City. The small Presbyterian church on the corner of East Main Street and South Street in Oyster Bay did not quite measure up to their idea of what a church should be. In 1866, they arranged to have their cousin, Reverend Benjamin Lincoln Swan, take over the pastorate of the Oyster Bay church in order to hopefully revitalize the congregation. Reverend Swan was born in Medford, Massachusetts, on July 31, 1813. He attended Harvard College but did not graduate, and he received an honorary degree from Yale University in 1844. He was ordained as a pastor of the

Presbyterian Church in Fair Haven, Connecticut, in 1836 and was installed as the pastor of a church in Litchfield, Connecticut, in 1846. Edward Swan took a leading role in having the church built along with his younger brother, Otis Swan, and each of them contributed substantial sums to make the new church possible. The new church, designed by the noted church architect J. Cleveland Cady, was dedicated on September 23, 1873. The Swans had been members of the Union League Club of New York City along with the Roosevelts, who were also members of the Fifth Avenue Presbyterian Church. Theodore Roosevelt Sr., the father of the president, also became very active in the building of the new church and served as an elder until his death in 1878.

Otis Swan did not live on Cove Neck with his two older brothers. Instead, he lived with his father, Benjamin Lincoln Swan Jr., in New York City until his father's death in January 1866. In April 1867, he married Charlotte Anthon, who died shortly after on July 22, 1869. After his wife's death, Otis summered in a house on Cove Road that he rented from Smith Thompson Van Buren, the son of President Martin Van Buren. In 1874, Otis Swan moved out of the house on Cove Road, which was then rented to Theodore Roosevelt Sr. On November 11, 1876, Otis Dwight Swan married Sarah M. Weed at the First Presbyterian Church in Oyster Bay. Doc Wightman recorded in his diary that he went over to the wedding "in a drenching rain" but that the church was still very crowded. Little more than a month later, the news broke that Otis Swan had defalcated on funds entrusted to him, and he disappeared from town. He was not heard from again until he turned up in Emporia, Kansas, in July 1878. It was discovered that he had reestablished his law practice and regained his reputation. He became a trustee of Emporia College and was known in Kansas as Judge Swan. Otis died in Emporia on March 26, 1894.

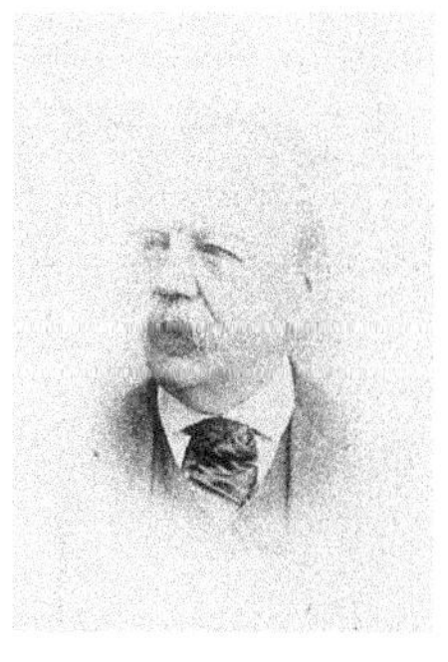

Unlike his brothers, Otis Swan did not buy land on Cove Neck. He did rent the place on Cove Road known as *Tranquility*, which was later rented by Theodore Roosevelt Sr. and his family. *Courtesy of the Oyster Bay Historical Society.*

Celebrating the Fourth of July was a big deal for the Swan family. Each year, Edward Swan had one of his hired men put aside brushwood and fallen trees on the beach in front of his house. As soon as evening darkened the skies, the huge bonfire of collected brushwood would be lit to the delight of the people in the village who could view it from across the bay. All of the children from Cove Neck and the Cove would be gathered around, watching the house-sized fire as they played games. The bonfire spectacles would be supplemented by fireworks that lasted long into the evening. Mary Fanny Youngs wrote about the beauty of the reflections of the fireworks and bonfire on the waters of the Cove: "The rockets' red glare, and the shooting stars of the Roman candles, and the whizzing of Catherine wheels, reflected in the still, dark water of the harbor was a sight from Fairyland. Oh, the Fourth of July was the very day of days!" On August 30, 1903, Edward H. Swan died at age seventy-five at his Cove Neck home, where his wife also died on September 28, 1907.

WILLIAM "BILLY" LINCOLN SWAN INHERITS BENJAMIN LINCOLN SWAN JR. PROPERTY

In 1892, Benjamin Lincoln Swan Jr., father of Commodore William Lincoln Swan, died. His wife, Mary Rhinelander Renwick Swan, died at age eighty in May 1901, at her home at 5 West Twentieth Street, New York City. The *Woodside Farms* property in Cove Neck was then inherited in 1902 by her stepson, William Lincoln Swan. In September 1871, William Lincoln Swan invited some of his local yachting friends to a meeting aboard his forty-foot yacht, *Glance*, while it was anchored off Soper's Point, Centre Island. The purpose of the meeting was to interest them in forming a new yacht club. After several more meetings were held, a charter was signed on December 30, 1871, forming the Seawanhaka Corinthian Yacht Club. Swan was elected as the club's first commodore. Within a few years, the Seawanhaka Yacht Club relocated to Staten Island, and Billy Swan, Cornelius Roosevelt and Hilborne Roosevelt, along with others who were only interested in racing closer to home, organized the Oyster Bay Yacht Club in 1885. The two clubs were later reunited in 1892. Commodore Swan, as he was known around the village, was a lawyer, trained at Columbia Law School, with many other talents. He loved to sail and enjoyed the company of his crew, with whom he liked nothing better than to spend an evening singing sea chanties and drinking from a bottle of rum. He was also an accomplished organist and played the Hilborne Roosevelt organ, which he donated to the First Presbyterian Church at Oyster Bay, for over fifty years before he relocated to Baltimore, Maryland, in 1923. He was also a profuse grower of flowers and had a greenhouse erected behind his home on Cove Road, which he had purchased from John A. Weeks in August 1887.

On August 24, 1881, William Lincoln Swan married Isabel (Belle) Thurston at the First Presbyterian Church in Oyster Bay. She was the daughter of William Thurston, a cobbler who ran a shop on South Street in Oyster Bay and lived in a modest house on Hamilton Avenue. The Swan family protested the marriage from the moment William announced his engagement. Although invitations were sent to all members of the Swan family, not a single member of the family attended. The wedding was heavily attended by the Thurstons, the servants of the summer community and village folk. The wedding caused a considerable stir in the community, as many thought William had married out of his class. The couple was shunned by the Oyster Bay summer community for many years, and Commodore Swan was cut off from his family and friends, who refused to have anything to do with him or his wife. Swan's father opened the door to reconciliation when he finally reinstated William's claim to his inheritance. A short time after, the matter was finally resolved when Frank Underhill invited the Swans to a ball given at his mansion in July 1889. Mrs. Swan was reported to have been elegantly dressed and was in every way the equal of all the other women at the ball.

In June 1902, William Lincoln Swan wrote to Theodore Roosevelt offering the use of the dock at *Woodside Farm* to the president's wife, Edith, when she arrived at Oyster Bay in the presidential yacht *Dolphin*. He explained in the letter that the dock was the only Cove Neck dock that was directly on the highway and, as such, would be the most convenient when meeting guests by carriage. He added that the dock would also be at the president's disposal for the entire summer season. He signed his letter "yours sincerely and fraternally," which was a reference to the bond they shared in Matinecock Lodge. Swan had been the founder of Matinecock Lodge in 1892, and he had invited Roosevelt to become a member at a dinner in his former home on East Main Street in November 1898, shortly after Roosevelt was elected governor of New York. Roosevelt declined at that time, believing that he would be too busy with the affairs of the State. However, in 1900, shortly after becoming the elected vice-president of the United States, Roosevelt believed he would have more time on his hands and accepted his membership.

On October 13, 1917, Elizabeth Swan, daughter of William Lincoln Swan, married Henry Fuller Howden. The wedding was performed at *Woodside Farm*, the home of William Lincoln Swan. The 230 guests were met at the railroad station with special cars, which transported them to the scene of the wedding. The ceremony was performed by Reverend Harry S. Dunning of the First Presbyterian Church of Oyster Bay and Reverend W.

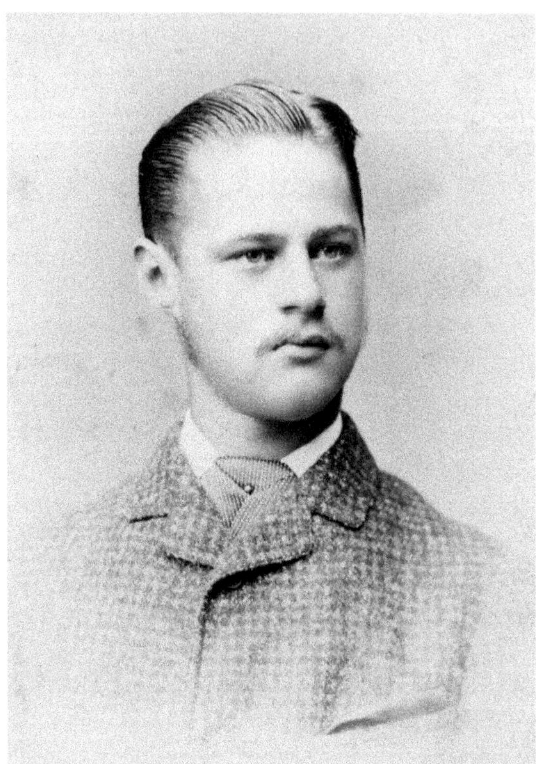

Left: Frank Underhill was the first from Oyster Bay to open his doors to Billy Swan and his new bride, Belle Thurston, and welcome them into local society. Frank Underhill also partnered with Theodore Roosevelt in establishing a polo team in Oyster Bay. *Courtesy of John Hammond.*

Below: The presidential yacht *Mayflower* was brought to Oyster Bay most summers. It was aboard the *Mayflower* that Theodore Roosevelt hosted the Russian and Japanese delegations, which led to his receiving the Nobel Peace Prize. *Courtesy John Hammond.*

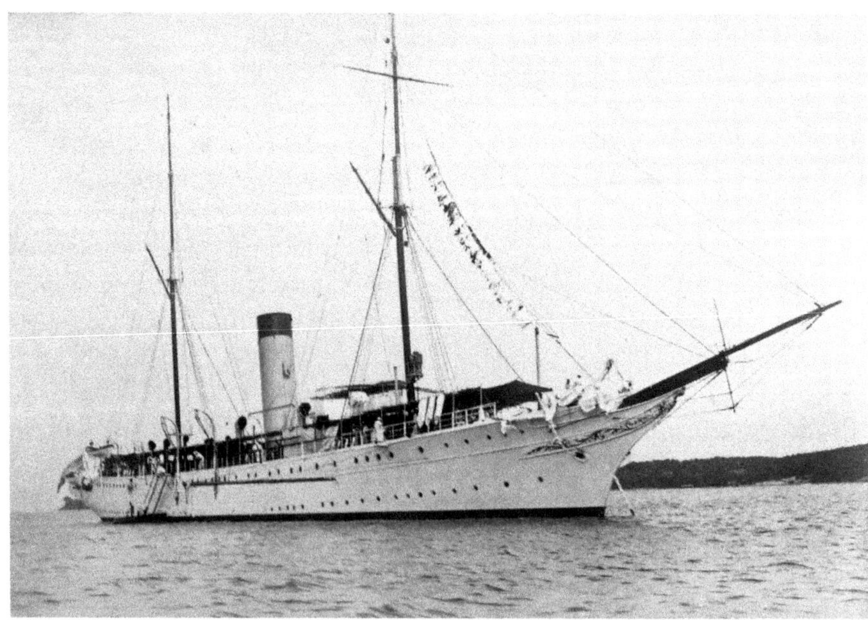

Scott Stiles of Wilkes-Barre, Pennsylvania. Reverend Stiles was a member of the class of 1869 at Princeton, as was Billy Swan. The newly married couple made their home in Baltimore, Maryland.

In November 1924, Billy Swan resigned his position as organist of the First Presbyterian Church, sold his East Main Street home to Dr. Minor C. Hill and moved to Baltimore to take up residence with his daughter. He did not sell the *Woodside Farm* property, but he did rent it to Colonel Theodore Roosevelt Jr. On October 31, 1925, Swan wrote to Leslie E. Bushnell that he greatly regretted that he would be unable to attend the special meeting of Matinecock Lodge. In the letter, he said, "I have been under the weather for the past three months, with a lame knee and heart trouble." Eight days later, on November 8, 1925, at age seventy-eight, Billy Swan died in Baltimore. His widow, Isabel Thurston Swan, died at age eighty-seven on May 21, 1942.

VanSantvoord Merle-Smith

Following the deaths of Edward Swan in 1903 and his wife in 1907, the *Evergreens* property was rented out by the family to VanSantvoord Merle-Smith for several summers. Merle-Smith later bought the property in 1921 and renamed it the *Paddocks*. Van Santvoord Merle-Smith was born in Sea Bright, New Jersey, on June 22, 1889. He graduated from Princeton in 1911 and from Harvard Law School in 1914. In 1916, he married Kate Grosvenor Fowler, with whom he had four children: VanSantvoord Jr., born in 1917; Nancy, born in 1921; Fowler, born in 1926; and Margaret, born in 1929. Merle-Smith enlisted in the New York National Guard in 1914 as a corporal and served until 1917, when he was transferred to the 165th Infantry and sent to France. During Merle-Smith's time in France, his unit commander was killed in action and he took command of his unit. After taking command, he was wounded by a rifle shot to his right elbow on July 28, 1918. For his actions, Merle-Smith was awarded the Distinguished Service Cross and he was discharged as a major on May 7, 1919. He later became the third assistant secretary of state and served in that position from June 24, 1920, to March 4, 1921. He then went to work for the New York Law firm of Pratt & McAlpin, where he became a successful investment banker. During the breakup of Roosevelt & Son in 1933, Merle-Smith became head of one of the three branch companies that was formed.

Merle-Smith was reactivated as a colonel at the beginning of World War II, and he became the executive intelligence officer for General Douglas MacArthur in the South Pacific. In August 1943, he suffered a mental breakdown from the pressures of the work and was sent back to Cove Neck. He died three months later on November 9, 1943, from acute cardiac failure, which was attributed to the wartime pressures he had been under. He was buried in Menands, New York, but in 1965, his body was removed, cremated and reburied in Keene Valley, New York.

10

JAMES STUART BLACKTON

A notable architectural feature for most of the twentieth century on Cove Neck was known to several generations of local residents as the Leeds Boathouse. It stood on the shore of Cold Spring Harbor from 1914 to 1983, when its remains were razed. Although it was commonly known as the Leeds Boathouse, the structure wasn't actually built by Billy Leeds but by a much earlier owner of the property, James Stuart Blackton.

James Stuart Blackton was born in Sheffield, England, on January 4, 1875. Blackton's father died when he was only an infant, and his mother took the family to America in August 1886. They sailed from Liverpool, England, aboard the SS *Celtic* and settled in a small house in the Morrisania section of the Bronx. Blackton began his career as a carpenter's apprentice at age eleven, despite his childhood dreams of being an artist or a person in show business. His childhood dream began to materialize when he met two men named Albert E. Smith and Ronald Reader. In 1894, they met at a boardinghouse run by Reader, who was an amateur magician employed by the Royal Insurance Company. During his time at the boardinghouse, Blackton developed his ability to draw cartoons by making magic lantern (a device used for showing slides, either photographic or hand-drawn, by projecting them onto a screen) slides for Reader. Reader, Smith and Blackton later formed a Lyceum act billed as "The Celebrated Reader, Smith and Blackton Combination." Smith was billed as the Komical Konjurer, Blackton as the Komical Kartoonist and Reader operated an early version of the magic lantern, using many of Blackton's artistic slides. The act was

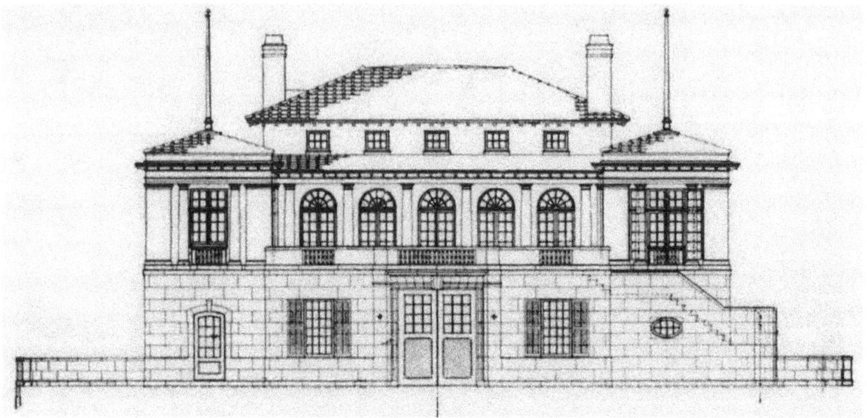

The architectural plan for the Blackton Boathouse. *Courtesy of the Griffin family.*

not a great success, so Reader soon went back to the insurance business, Smith took a job as a bookbinder and Blackton took a job as a cub reporter for the *New York Evening World*.

On April 22, 1896, Blackton was asked by the *New York Evening World* to conduct an interview with Thomas Alva Edison about his new projecting machine. Although the interview started slowly, mainly due to Edison's near deafness, Blackton was able to strike up a friendship with Edison when he demonstrated his ability to draw cartoons. Edison asked Blackton to draw a sketch of him, which he did, and it reportedly pleased Edison greatly. After he completed the drawing, Blackton asked Edison if he could buy one of the newly developed projecting machines, to which Edison agreed, and Blackton placed an order for one on the spot. A few months later, Blackton accepted the delivery of an Edison projecting kinetoscope, which cost him $800. Blackton then joined up with his former partner, Albert E. Smith, and formed the American Vitagraph Company in 1896.

Smith and Blackton began making short films, mainly for the same Lyceum and vaudeville clients that their defunct act had previously served. They purchased additional Edison projectors, but the business was not very successful. Their big break came with the Spanish-American War, when Blackton produced a film titled *Tearing Down the Spanish Flag*, which was the first motion picture to ever depict war. The film whipped up a lot of patriotic fervor and resulted in many young men immediately signing up to fight. Albert Smith followed *Tearing Down the Spanish Flag* with a film that showed the burials of some of the casualties from the USS *Maine* at

Arlington National Cemetery. At that time, William Randolph Hearst was chartering a ship to take newspaper correspondents to Cuba to cover the war. Smith and Blackton were able to book passage on the chartered ship with a new projector system, developed by Smith, called the Dunderberger. Smith and Blackton used the Dunderberger to film Theodore Roosevelt and his Rough Riders at Kettle and San Juan Hills, which became the first war news film ever taken. For the first time, motion picture film was used not only to incite patriotic fervor but also to bring firsthand accounts of international events to the public.

With the success of their war films, Smith and Blackton took on a new partner in 1899. William T. Rock, or "Pop" Rock, as he came to be known, was also of English birth, having been born in Birmingham, England, on December 31, 1853. He was many years older than both Smith and Blackton and had the maturity of years that his junior partners lacked. When the company was incorporated in 1900, Pop Rock was named as president of American Vitagraph Corporation, Albert E. Smith was named as treasurer and J. Stuart Blackton was named as secretary. The new partnership became very successful over the next decade, producing hundreds of novelty films as well as pioneering the filming of documentaries, which covered many events, including the 1900 Galveston, Texas flood, the 1905 inauguration of President Theodore Roosevelt and the 1906 San Francisco earthquake. In 1905, the company bought property in Brooklyn and constructed a new film studio in 1906, which cost $25,000. In 1909, Blackton and three assistants were given special places at the inauguration of President William Howard Taft in order to film the ceremony. Two days after the inauguration, Vitagraph released film footage from the event. The vaudeville market for films was replaced by nickelodeon viewers (machines, usually located in arcades, where customers could pay a nickel to view a short movie), which sprang up throughout the country. By 1910, Vitagraph was releasing three reels of film each week for the nickelodeon market and employed a full-time staff of actors, technical staff and seven directors, earning the company a profit of over $600,000 a year. By 1912, Vitagraph had over four hundred employees.

Smith, Blackton and Pop Rock each became wealthy beyond their wildest dreams. In 1908, Blackton bought a fifty-foot steam yacht named the *Runaway* and joined the prestigious Atlantic Yacht Club. Blackton later replaced the *Runaway* with the *Paula,* which became the flagship of the Atlantic Yacht Club. In 1912, he was elected commodore of the club and was thereafter referred to as Commodore Blackton. Commodore Blackton continued to seek out the largest of yachts and sold the *Paula* to replace it with the 250-foot *Sagamore*, no doubt named after his famous neighbor, Theodore Roosevelt's, estate. He also got bitten by the speedboat racing bug when he purchased his first speedboats, the *Vita I* and *Vita II*. He attained speeds of over forty miles an hour in 1911 and created a sensation in the sporting pages of the nation's newspapers. His second wife, Paula Hunt, who was born in Adairsville, Georgia, was also bitten by the bug and became an accomplished speedboat racer in her own right. Mrs. Blackton used one of the high-powered speed boats to chase down an invading shark in July 1916. She and two of her children, Charles and Violet, were down by the beach at Laurelton when Mrs. Blackton spied what she later described as an eight-foot-long shark with a blue-black body. She immediately got her children out of the water and shouted to alert other nearby swimmers. After reporting the incident to Charles Weeks, the Oyster Bay town clerk, Mrs. Blackton got into one of her speedboats and chased the creature down. Her neighbor, Louis Tiffany, assigned two of his employees to patrol the area but neither Mrs. Blackton nor the Tiffany employees saw the creature again. Blackton and his wife launched a period of breaking every known speedboat record and amassed a sizeable collection of sterling silver trophies. The trophies would come in handy many years later when Blackton's fortune disappeared.

Each of the three partners had grown up in poverty, keenly aware of the British class system. Blackton, although an easygoing person when he was producing films, was a social climber and sought the status he felt he deserved in society. Blackton's daughter Marian Constance Blackton wrote that her mother suggested that their family needed "an estate, a big estate, on Long Island, where the Best People have their homes." Blackton could think of no better place to settle than Cove Neck on Long Island, called by some New York newspapers the "Newport of Long Island." In 1912, Blackton sought to purchase a large tract of land in Cove Neck from Commodore William Lincoln Swan, the founder of the Seawanhaka Corinthian Yacht Club. The land was a part of *Woodside Farms* and stretched from Oyster Bay Harbor, across Cove Neck, to Cold Spring Harbor. On this property, his neighbors would include former president Theodore Roosevelt and Louis Comfort Tiffany. Blackton's daughter wrote, "Teddy Roosevelt on one side, the Tiffanys on the other. That's what Free Enterprise can bring to a self-made man in the good old USA."

Even before closing on the property, Blackton commissioned the noted architect Francis I.V. Hoppin to design his estate, which became known

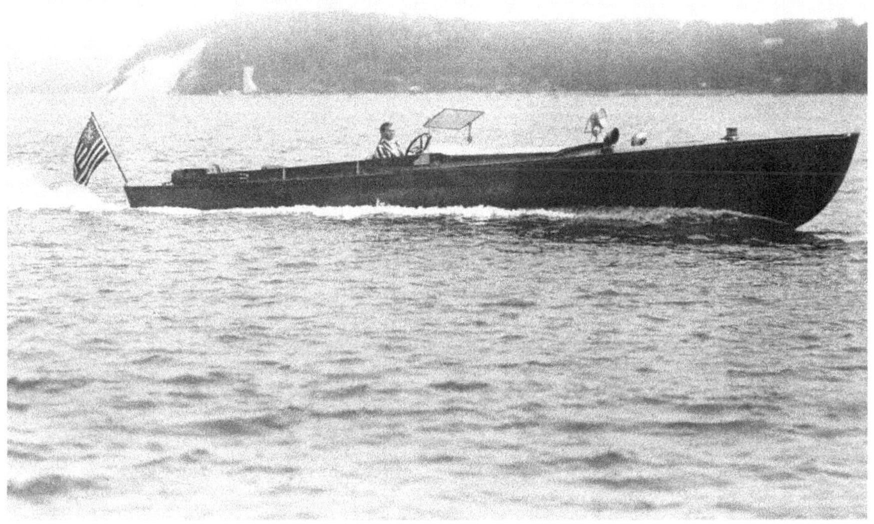

Albert E. Smith, treasurer of American Vitagraph Corporation and resident of Centre Island off of Cove Neck. In the background is Cooper's Bluff. *Courtesy of the Oyster Bay Historical Society.*

as *Harbourwood*, in the English fashion. Hoppin had graduated from the Massachusetts Institute of Technology and had been an apprentice architect with McKim, Mead and White of New York City. Hoppin had designed the award-winning Roslyn War Memorial, renovations to FDR's home at Hyde Park and many large homes in Newport. The initial plan was to build a cottage, supporting farm buildings and a boathouse. These structures were to be followed by the construction of a manse on the hill overlooking Cold Spring Harbor, just above the planned boathouse. The manse was to rival the largest and most ornate of all the best estates on the North Shore.

The sale of the land from William Lincoln Swan to James Stuart Blackton was closed on January 15, 1913, for the sum of $163,870. Blackton immediately applied to the Oyster Bay Town Board for the right to build a boathouse and channel leading to it. On March 24, 1913, Blackton received permission from the Oyster Bay Town Board to erect his planned boathouse and to dredge a 10-foot-deep channel surrounded by a 150-foot-long seawall

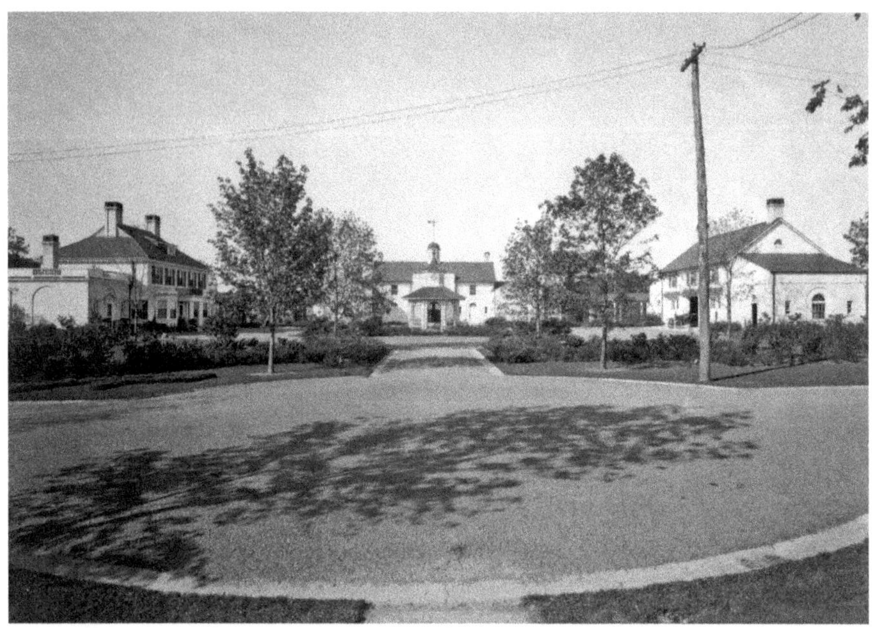

Harbourwood was built in 1915 by James Stuart Blackton. His plans for a mansion overlooking Cold Spring Harbor never materialized. *Courtesy John Hammond.*

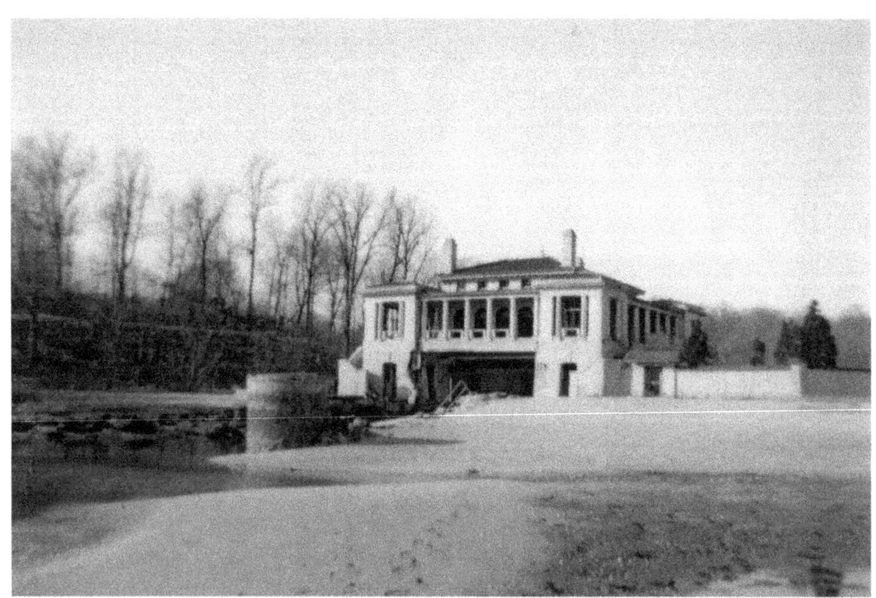

The creek was dredged out to provide continuous access to the water to and from the boathouse regardless of the tides. *Courtesy of the Griffin family.*

and dock. The lease agreement specified that rental for use of the property, which belonged to the Town of Oyster Bay, was set at $100 per year. At the end of the fifty-year term of the lease, the property was to revert back to the ownership of the town.

Construction of the boathouse began in 1913 and was completed in 1914, along with the dredging of the channel and the seawalls. The reinforced concrete boathouse was a remarkable structure, patterned after the seaside villas of Italy and built in the Renaissance Revival style. With its ornate tile roofs, the boathouse resembled a casino more than a boathouse. It was one of the largest of its kind and was considered to be the largest privately owned boathouse in the country. Dozens of Palladian French doors opened onto the verandas. At the water level, Blackton's Harmsworth Trophy–winning speedboats would pass under a lionhead keystone at the center of a cavernous archway as they entered the boathouse. In the channel, along the seawall, Blackton stored his large pleasure yachts. The second floor of the boathouse contained a large ballroom with a red-and-white, circus-style tented ceiling and massive fireplaces at each end. The boathouse also contained several rooms for the servants and crew members of Blackton's yachts.

One of the local families that lived in the boathouse was that of Charles (Charlie) Henry Griffin, who was born in Sayville on June 17, 1884. Charlie came to Oyster Bay to find work around 1900, and, shortly after, met and married Amelia Remsen Smith, daughter of Daniel Dykeman Smith, who had brought electricity to Oyster Bay in 1891 when he built the hydroelectric plant at the Mill Pond. Charlie Smith worked as a carpenter and handyman for Blackton, while his wife worked as a domestic servant. The arrangement was very satisfactory for the Griffin family, and they even named one of their children Violet after Blackton's daughter Violet Virginia Blackton. The Griffins lived in a boathouse apartment from 1917 to 1926.

Blackton's *Harbourwood* estate and the boathouse were used for many Vitagraph films, and the crews were often brought out to Cove Neck. In 1916, Blackton got special permission from the Brooklyn Society for the Prevention of Cruelty to Children to use ten-year-old Dorothy Farrier and fourteen-year-old Victor Norman in his film *The Chattel*, which was filmed in Cove Neck between June 21 and June 24, 1916. The boathouse also became the scene of many lavish parties as Blackton sought out the social recognition he felt he had earned. But his parties were generally shunned by the most socially prominent families of the North Shore of Long Island.

Just across the bay from Cove Neck, Blackton's longtime partner and the first president of Vitagraph, Albert E. Smith, bought the George Bullock property, *The Folly*, in 1913. *The Folly* was a just to the south of Seawanhaka Corinthian Yacht Club. Smith also had a boathouse, but it was much smaller than Blackton's and was built to resemble the aft section of a Spanish galleon. Meyer and MacKay wrote in their 1976 book *History of Centre Island* that the boathouse had been a prop for one of the Vitagraph productions and was transferred to Centre Island after they were done shooting the film. In its later years, the prop was mainly used for parties.

In 1914, the plans for Blackton's manse on the hill were necessarily put on hold as war broke out in Europe. Blackton was very concerned with the events in Europe when he met Hudson Maxim, author of *Defenseless America*, in 1915. Blackton's discussions with Maxim inspired him to put the patriotic ideas from *Defenseless America* into a motion picture. These discussions also inspired Blackton to file a Declaration of Intention for Naturalization on June 14, 1915, to become an American citizen. Blackton followed through with the intention and filed a Petition for Naturalization exactly three years later on June 14, 1918.

Blackton had become friendly with his neighbor, Theodore Roosevelt, when he filmed the Rough Riders in Cuba. After moving to Cove Neck, Blackton went over to *Sagamore Hill* to discuss his ideas for a patriotic film with Roosevelt. According to his autobiography, Blackton said to Roosevelt, "I intend to make a motion picture showing what would happen if this country was invaded by an enemy army. I am going to put the facts before the American public and try to arouse them to an awareness of their danger." After hearing Blackton's ideas, Roosevelt took a Bible from his bookcase and reportedly said to Blackton, "Here it is, the thirty-third chapter of Ezekiel, third verse; 'Whosoever heareth the sound of the trumpet and heedeth not, if the sword comes and takes him away, his blood shall be upon his own head.' That's America today. Heedless! Put that in your picture Blackton." Roosevelt then put Blackton in touch with Admiral Dewey, Reverend Lyman Abbott, Elihu Root and Major General Leonard Wood to gain information for his movie, which was to be called *Battle Cry of Peace*. Dewey, Abbott, Wood and Maxim all appeared in the movie with their words in subtitles. Roosevelt declined to appear, as he felt doing so might be interpreted as a bid on his part to seek the 1916 presidential nomination.

Battle Cry of Peace was first viewed on August 6, 1915, at the Vitagraph Theatre in New York City. On September 9, 1915, it was released to theaters across the country. The film played to rave reviews and was endorsed by civic and religious leaders. The Daughters of the American Revolution (DAR) arranged a special viewing for Congress and even invited President Woodrow

Wilson, but Wilson declined to attend. Henry Ford publicly opposed the film, claiming in the *New York Mail*'s December 11, 1915 edition that it was made by militant propagandists who were financially connected with munitions plants. Vitagraph sued Ford for libel and received a judgement in its favor on April 23, 1917, from the New York Federal District Court. The greatest review for *Battle Cry of Peace* came from Roosevelt himself, according to Blackton's daughter Marian Blackton Trimble. She wrote in her biography of her father that in a speech Theodore Roosevelt delivered in Madison Square Garden on July 6, 1916, he said, "Blackton has done more for the cause of Preparedness with his *Battle Cry of Peace* than any living man." Coming from a very proud daughter and long after the actual events we must take this statement with a grain of salt.

Roosevelt addressed the residents of Oyster Bay about their responsibilities as citizens from the bandstand at Townsend Park on the occasion of the annual Fourth of July parade in 1916. James Stuart Blackton was selected as the grand marshal of the parade, which was sponsored by the Oyster Bay Businessmen's Association. Blackton brought the Vitagraph film crew to the parade; cameramen were located at several points around the village to take extensive footage of the entire parade and the speech by Theodore Roosevelt. In October 1916, the finished film was shown to Oyster Bay residents at the Lyric Theatre on Audrey Avenue to a packed house. Many clips of that film still survive today, including the footage of Roosevelt giving his speech from the bandstand.

Early in 1917, Blackton left Vitagraph to become an independent film producer, but he retained his stock ownership in the company. He began making artistically inspired films based on classical literature, and he believed there was a strong market for this type of film. Blackton's independent film production efforts were a failure, and his position of wealth and status began to erode. When the United States finally entered World War I in 1917, Blackton turned over the largest of his private yachts to the navy. He also aided the war effort by joining the Atlantic Flying Boat Squadron, of which he was named commodore. The mission of the squadron was to develop aerial photography techniques. Blackton also produced many training films for the military, which included films on hand-to-hand combat and artillery maneuvers, and they normally ended with shots of armed doughboys marching straight toward the camera. These films were frequently sent to U.S. troops in Europe and to other Allied countries. In December 1917, one of Blackton's films, *The Judgement House*, was released. It was the last of his films to contain scenes shot at *Harbourwood*, his Cove Neck home. The film was described by his daughter Marian as mediocre and did poorly at the box office.

Blackton Sells to Frank Strachan

On June 20, 1918, James Stuart Blackton sold the *Harbourwood* estate at Cove Neck to Frank Duncan M. Strachan from Brunswick, Georgia. The terms of the sale included not only the boathouse and the farm buildings but even the horses, cattle, other livestock, furniture, tools, equipment and anything else that remained on the property at the time of sale. The sale also included the boats that remained on the premises after the larger vessels were given to the navy.

Frank Duncan M. Strachan was born in Banff, Scotland, in 1871 to Frank G. Strachan, who had founded the Strachan Shipping Company in Brunswick, Georgia, in 1886. The company was a major stevedoring operation, which controlled stevedoring for the ports along the Gulf of Mexico and for the South Atlantic ports of the United States. At the end of the First World War, Frank Strachan was named as a member of a committee to form the Emergency Fleet Corporation in February 1919. It was the task of this committee to devise a plan for the disposal of the many merchant and private ships that had been taken into naval service during the war.

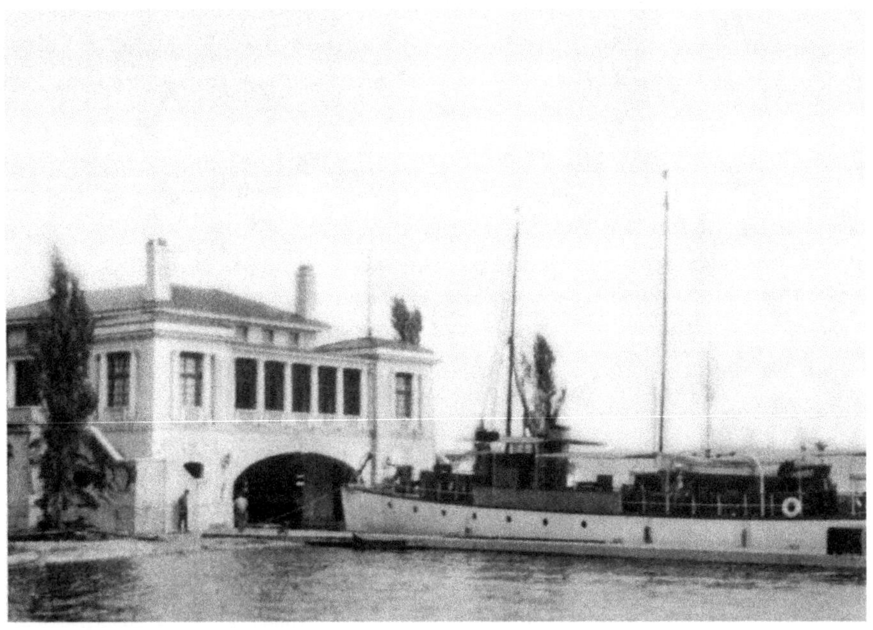

Blackton sold the property to Strachan, who brought up some of his boats from Georgia. This one was the *Vamoose* from Brunswick, Georgia. *Courtesy of the Griffin family.*

Frank Strachan didn't make any changes to the *Harbourwood* property, and he even retained the Griffin family, who lived in the boathouse. Although Strachan brought several of his yachts from Brunswick, Georgia, to Oyster Bay each summer, his lifestyle was somewhat subdued compared to that of flamboyant movie mogul J. Stuart Blackton. However, it was during the period of Strachan's ownership of the property that the roadway now known as Tennis Court Road was paved. The plan was to pave the path with trap rock and cover it with Tarvia binder, completing what was known as a macadam surface. In October 1921, bids were received from several local contractors to grade the pathway that led from Cove Neck Road to the shore of Cold Spring Harbor.

Strachan Sells to Leeds

On September 30, 1926, Frank Strachan, who was still listing his address as Brunswick, Georgia, sold *Harbourwood* to William Bateman Leeds Jr. Leeds may have heard of the intended sale of the Strachan property while he was on St. Simons Island, one of his favorite vacation spots near Brunswick, Georgia. William Bateman Leeds Jr. was born in New York City on September 19, 1902, to May Stewart and William Bateman Leeds. When Billy Leeds was only six years old, his father died in Paris, France, leaving a fortune of $35 million to Billy and his mother, which he had amassed through his financial success in tin plating and marketing. May Stewart Leeds remained in Europe, socializing with the European aristocracy, following the death of her husband. In 1914. May's engagement to Prince Christopher of Greece and Denmark was announced in Biarritz, France; however, the marriage did not take place until February 1, 1920, in Vevey, Switzerland. Following the marriage to Prince Christopher, May became known as Princess Anastasia of Greece. Shortly after becoming Princess Anastasia, May was diagnosed with cancer and died in 1923. Her remains were interred at Woodlawn Cemetery in the Bronx. William Bateman Leeds Jr. had inherited an estimated $7 million upon the death of his father in 1908, when Billy Leeds was six years old, but he became fabulously wealthy upon receiving the inheritance left by his mother, Princess Anastasia.

Billy Leeds was living with his mother in Europe when, in 1921, he married Princess Xenia Georgievna Romanov of Russia, cousin of the czar and niece of his mother's husband, Prince Christopher. Princess Xenia was born on August 22, 1903, in Russia and was the daughter of Grand Duke George Mikhailovich, who had been executed by firing squad in St. Petersburg in 1919. Billy Leeds's mother was reported to have had serious objections to the marriage due to the age of the couple; Billy Leeds was only nineteen, and his bride was eighteen. On February 25, 1925, William Bateman Leeds and Princess Xenia became the parents of a daughter, Nancy Helen Marie Leeds.

On September 30, 1926, Billy Leeds bought the estate of Frank D.M. Strachan at Cove Neck and immediately changed the name of the estate to *Kenwood*. Although they had an infant daughter, Billy Leeds and Princess Xenia led a wild lifestyle of Gatsby-era parties. At a time when North Shore Long Island parties had quite the reputation for being extravagant, the parties of the Leedses stood above others in their intensity and duration, often lasting several days. On a lark, in May 1927, Billy Leeds sailed to Europe with no passport or luggage. He explained to the press that he had been visiting a business associate who was supposed to represent him at a conference in Paris, but when the businessman failed to show up at the ship, the *Aquitania*, Leeds decided to go to Paris himself and stayed on the ship.

Princess Xenia got herself into the middle of the controversy surrounding Anna Anderson in 1927. Anna Anderson was a woman who claimed to be Grand Duchess Anastasia, who had reportedly been executed along with her entire family, including her father, the czar of Russia. Xenia contacted Anna and invited her to *Kenwood*, believing that if Anna was, in fact, an imposter, she would be in a position to prevent any adverse publicity for the family. Xenia also believed that if Anna was who she claimed to be, it would be a ghastly thing to leave her alone in the world against all of her critics. Anna Anderson came to live at *Kenwood*, where Xenia came to believe Anna's story and they became fast friends. Xenia claimed she immediately recognized her upon meeting her, although Xenia had only been nine years old when she last saw Anastasia. However, Xenia clung to her belief that Anna Anderson was the grand duchess even after she was thrown out of *Kenwood* by Billy Leeds.

Billy Leeds had an intense interest in aviation, and in August 1927, he flew from Garden City, Long Island, to Lake Placid, New York, in a tri-engine Fokker. A few weeks after that flight, Billy Leeds qualified for a private pilot's license. Leeds also ordered a special plane to be built for him in Ireland; it was to be a blue and white monoplane named *Princess Xenia*. Charles Lindbergh had become the first to fly solo across the Atlantic just a few months earlier, in May 1927, and Billy Leeds hoped that the *Princess Xenia* would become the first plane to make the flight from Europe to America. *Princess Xenia* took off with a pilot and copilot from Ballybunnion, Ireland, on September 16, but after fighting fierce headwinds and a blinding fog, the flight was aborted after only four and a half hours. The *Princess Xenia* did later make it to America and became Billy Leeds's personal airplane.

Early in 1927, Billy Leeds signed a contract with Johannes Plumm of Cold Spring Harbor for him to design a speedboat. The final boat was built in secrecy by Robert J. Purdy, a speedboat builder from Port Washington. In the fall of 1927, Purdy completed work on the boat, which Leeds named the *Fantail* after the radical design of the stern that resembled the tail flutes of a whale. The boat was equipped with two Wright Typhoon marine engines and was thirty-eight feet long and about nine feet wide. Billy Leeds was immensely proud of his new speedboat, and on November 20, 1927, he invited two dozen of his friends to witness and ride the *Fantail* as he took the boat out for its initial trial runs. What his invitees did not know was that the boat would be piloted by his wife, Princess Xenia. Among the guests were Prince Eric of Denmark, Prince Christopher of Greece and some naval attachés interested in the potential of the *Fantail* as a possible torpedo boat design. On the calm waters of Cold Spring Harbor, with twenty-four people on board, the *Fantail*, piloted by Princess Xenia, was clocked going 63.07 miles per hour.

The *Fantail* was, however, a little too fast for young Billy Leeds to control. Just one week after undergoing trial runs, Billy Leeds, Johannes Plumm, the *Fantail*'s designer and three guests were traveling to New York City when the *Fantail* struck a submerged log at a high rate of speed two miles off Sands Point. In the darkness, Leeds and Plumm tried to determine the scope of the damage, but they were unable to verify whether it would be safe to restart the engines, so they paddled the *Fantail* to shore. The *Fantail* was not seriously damaged, and after some repairs, it was placed back into service, but its troubles were not over.

On July 8, 1928, dancer Fred Astaire and his sister, Adele Astaire, who was a very popular stage actress, were guests at one of Billy Leeds's numerous parties at *Kenwood*. Billy Leeds invited them to go for a ride in the *Fantail* along with his wife. Billy Leeds and Adele Astaire climbed aboard and started the engines while Fred Astaire and Princess Xenia waited on shore. Unknown to Billy Leeds, some fuel had seeped into the bilge and was ignited when he started the engines. This caused a massive explosion, which immediately enveloped the boat in flames. Billy Leeds was credited with saving Adele Astaire's life by pulling her from the flaming *Fantail* as Fred Astaire and

Princess Xenia helplessly looked on. The Atlantic Steamer Fire Company responded to a call for assistance, but by the time they had arrived, the *Fantail* had burned to the waterline and was completely destroyed. Billy Leeds was treated for minor burns at his home, but Adele Astaire, who suffered more serious burns, had to be taken to New York Hospital. She eventually made a full recovery and returned to the stage and further stardom.

In August 1929, the German airship *Graf Zeppelin* left Lakehurst, New Jersey, on a voyage around the world. Aboard that flight was Billy Leeds, who had flown a tri-motor Fokker from Curtis Field in Garden City to join the *Graf Zeppelin*. The German airship had made its first flight on September 18, 1928, and was the largest of several hydrogen-filled airships. The trip originated from and returned to Lakehurst with only three stops in Friedrichshafen, Germany; Tokyo, Japan; and Los Angeles. The *Graf Zeppelin* was 237 meters (778 feet) long and had a top speed of 111 kilometers per hour (69 miles per hour). It continued in service for many years following its only trip around the world, but it was taken out of service following the spectacular explosion of its sister ship, *Hindenburg*, at Lakehurst in 1937.

In October 1929, Princess Xenia and her five-year-old daughter returned from a long visit to Europe. They sailed in on the *Mauretania* and were greeted in lower New York Bay by Billy Leeds in one of his powerful boats. The following month, Billy Leeds purchased the 165-foot steam yacht *Winchester* and immediately renamed it the *Flying Fox*. Over the next several years, Billy Leeds kept buying larger and larger yachts, which were capped off by his purchase of the 273-foot long *Moana*, which he purchased in 1936.

In February 1930, for reasons never publicly disclosed, Billy Leeds and Princess Xenia divorced. After the split, however, they remained amicable and occasionally appeared together at public events. A few months later, Billy Leeds had his yacht anchored off Atlantic City, New Jersey, when a young woman appeared to be in trouble in a small rowboat. Her name was Olive Hamilton, and she was rescued and brought aboard Leeds's yacht. She claimed that she had been trying to get a close-up look of the fantastic yacht, but some claim that she staged the scene. She was a twenty-four-year-old telephone operator, and Billy Leeds was smitten with her beauty. They soon became constant companions, and in 1936, they were married.

Billy Leeds lived principally aboard his various yachts from the time of his divorce, although he maintained an apartment in New York City. He began to neglect *Kenwood* and did not pay the taxes that were due. In May 1937, *Kenwood* was sold at auction for $160,000 to an unidentified buyer. The attorney for the purchaser, Joseph J. Lerner of Manhattan, would only say that he represented a man from the South who was a yachtsman and sportsman. It was later learned that Billy Leeds had purchased his own property back at the tax sale. However, he again fell behind in paying the taxes, and in 1939, Leeds owed the Village of Cove Neck $908.50. The property was finally acquired by Nassau County for nonpayment of taxes, and it sold the property in April 1945.

Princess Xenia remarried and lived the rest of her life in Glen Cove, New York, where she died on September 17, 1965, at the age of sixty-two. Billy Leeds spent most of the rest of his life traveling aboard his yachts until he was diagnosed with cancer in the 1970s. He died at his estate, *Wintersberg Peak*, on St. Thomas on December 31, 1971, from a self-inflicted gunshot wound.

11

THE ROOSEVELTS

When the name Roosevelt is mentioned, one immediately thinks of President Theodore Roosevelt, but as Dr. John Allen Gable, the late executive director of the Theodore Roosevelt Association, said in his foreword to the *Roosevelt Genealogy*, "To be sure, many Roosevelts were never known outside their social circles, and would not be noticed by later generations were it not for more famous relations." There were many Roosevelts other than the president who made Cove Neck their home. They usually followed a pattern of graduating from Harvard and entering military service before joining the family business, Roosevelt & Son, as partners. The history of the entire Roosevelt family is difficult to follow, due to the repetition of first and sometimes even middle names, so, it will be easier to deal with the history of the houses they built on Cove Neck.

The family had a curious custom of lining all the children up on special occasions to take photographs. Theodore Roosevelt wrote in his autobiography about the practice: "*Sagamore Hill* is one of three neighboring houses in which small cousins spent very happy years of childhood. In the three houses, there were at one time sixteen of these small cousins, all told, and once we ranged them in order of size and took their photograph." The photo he mentions was taken at *Sagamore Hill* in 1896 and shows the children of W. Emlen Roosevelt: Christine, George, Margaret, John and Philip; the children of Alfred Roosevelt: Elfreda, James and Katherine; Dr. J. West Roosevelt's children: Oliver, Nicholas and Lorraine; and Theodore Roosevelt's children: Alice, Theodore, Kermit, Ethel and Archie. In good

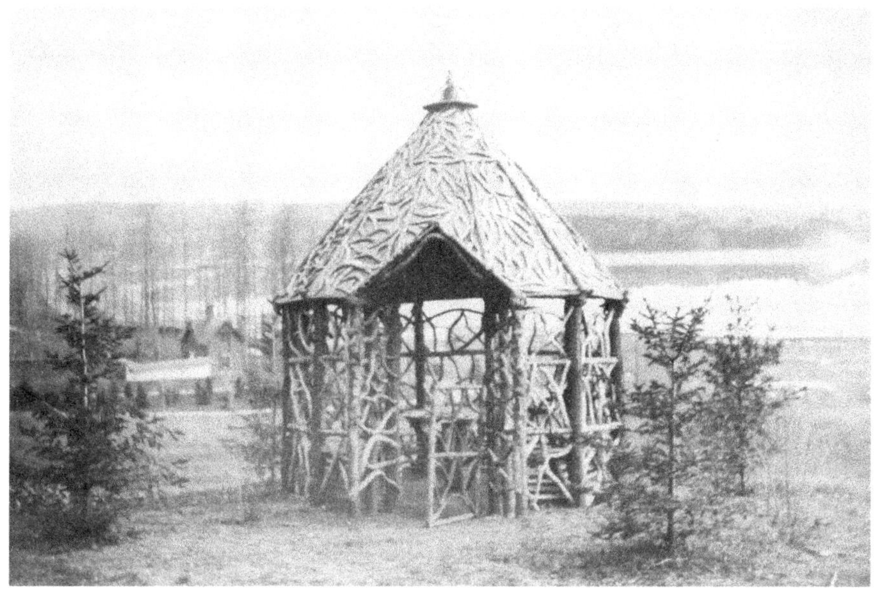

This summer house was on the grounds of *Gracewood*, the home of James K. Gracie, who had married the sister of Martha Bulloch, Theodore Roosevelt's mother. *Courtesy John Hammond.*

weather, the cousins would get together to picnic, swim, sail, row and play tennis at one of the two tennis courts at *Sagamore Hill* and *Yellowbanks*. They all knew how to ride horseback, and everyone had to learn to swim before they were allowed on the boat.

When the weather was bad, they would read, play chess and roughhouse in the family barns, and sometimes, the girls would organize amateur theatricals. Everyone memorized reams of poetry; some of the favorites were poems by Longfellow and Kipling. The family photograph of the children from 1908 shows the growth of some of the children from the 1896 photograph. Jack, George and Philip had grown over six feet tall, and their sisters, Christine and Margaret, had grown into young ladies. Theodore, Ethel, Archie and Quentin are in the picture, as are Oliver, Nick and Lorraine.

Elfreda had married in 1905 to Lord Orme Clark and had gone to live in Bibary Court, England. In 1909, both Christine and Katherine were married, Christine to an army officer she met on a visit to Cuba and Katherine to Stanley Reeve of Boston. Margaret died in 1914 after contracting typhoid on a trip to Brazil with Mrs. Theodore Roosevelt. In 1916, George married Julia Addison, and his brother John married Elise Weinacht. The First World War found many of the cousins engaged and far from Cove Neck. George

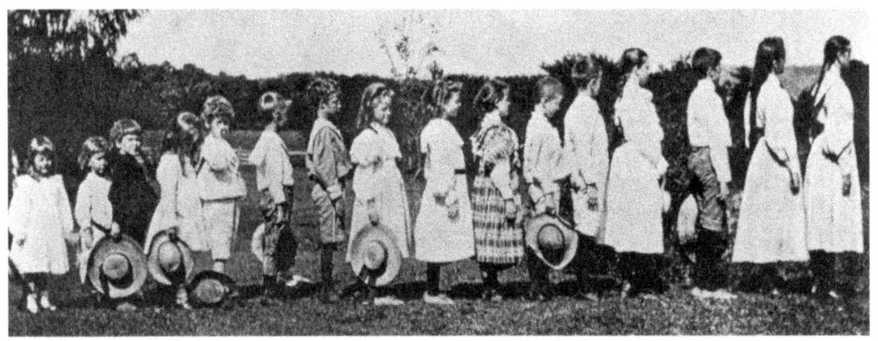

The sixteen Roosevelt cousins lined up according to height for this photograph in 1896. *Courtesy of Sagamore Hill National Historic Site.*

served in the army on the Mexican border against Pancho Villa. John became involved with the cable company, which the family had a financial interest in, and served in the signal corps before being transferred to the navy, where he spent a lot of time trying to get airplanes across the ocean to France. Philip and Quentin joined the air service and flew in France, where Quentin was killed, and Philip was awarded the Croix de Guerre. Theodore, Kermit and Archie all fought in the army.

After the war, many of the cousins married, and some moved away from Cove Neck. Those who remained produced additional generations who would spend their summers at Cove Neck. Theodore Roosevelt Jr. and his wife, Eleanor Butler Alexander, lived at *Gray Cottage* and *Woodside Farms* when they were not involved elsewhere. They later they built *Old Orchard* on the grounds of *Sagamore Hill*. Their son Quentin rented *Gray Cottage*, the ancestral home of the Coopers on Cove Neck, for a short time following World War II. Ethel married Dr. Richard Derby, and they lived on Lexington Avenue in Oyster Bay village with their four children. Archie and his wife, Gracie, moved to Cold Spring Harbor. George and Julia lived at *Gracewood*, just down the road from *Sagamore Hill*, which still had the family farm with cows, pigs and poultry up until World War II. Their children, Margaret, Medora, George and Julian, all grew up on Cove Neck. In 1925, Philip married his second cousin, Jean, who came from the South Shore. They were given the property on which they later built *Dolonor*. Their children, Philippa, P. James Jr. and John E., grew up there. P. James Jr. bought the old Youngs Homestead in 1952 for his first wife, Barbara.

The Roosevelts first came to Oyster Bay sometime before the Civil War, according to Frances Irvin. However, two decades would pass before any of

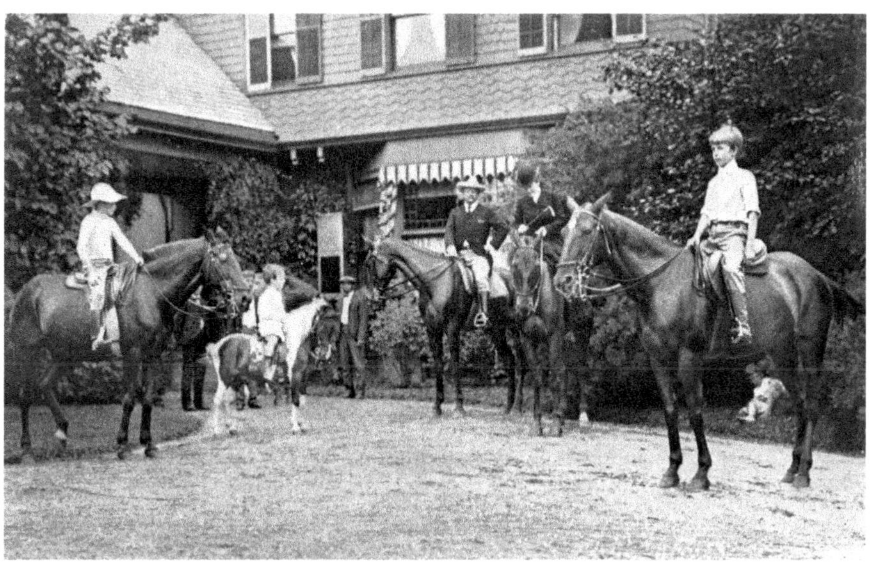

The Roosevelt family loved family rides on horseback around Cove Neck. This photo, taken before one of their rides, is from around 1907. *Courtesy Sagamore Hill National Historical Site.*

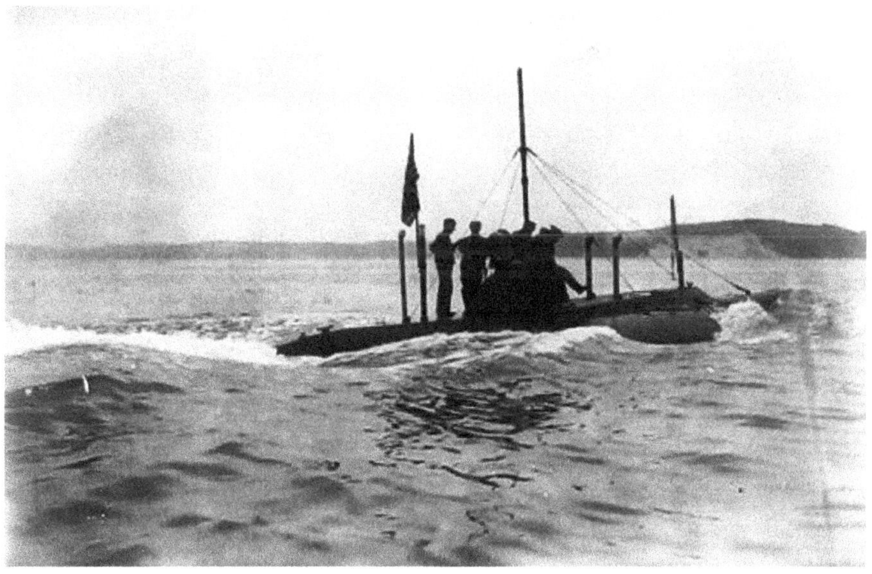

The U.S. Navy submarine *Plunger* on its way to Cove Neck in 1905. Theodore Roosevelt went down in the *Plunger* for over an hour off Cove Neck. *Courtesy of the US Navy.*

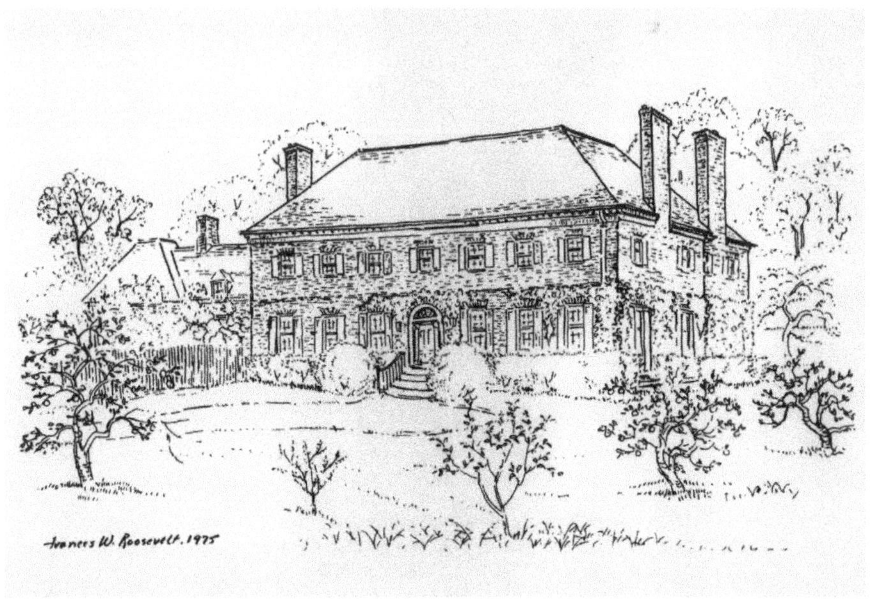

Frances Roosevelt made this drawing of her father-in-law, Theodore Roosevelt Jr.'s, home *Old Orchard. Courtesy Oyster Bay Historical Society.*

the family bought property there. On July 17, 1871, Cornelius van Schaack Roosevelt died at his summer home at Oyster Bay. He was born on January 30, 1794, and had attended Columbia College before leaving to join the family glass importing business in 1818. Cornelius joined the firm when it was renamed Roosevelt & Son. Upon the death of his father, James J. Roosevelt, in August 1840, Cornelius inherited the business. Through the business's income and keen real estate investments in Manhattan, Cornelius was able to amass a huge fortune, which placed him among the wealthiest men in New York. Cornelius married Margaret Barnhill in Philadelphia on October 9, 1821. Together, they had six sons, one of whom died in infancy. At the time of his death, in 1871, Cornelius was still head of Roosevelt & Son, despite the fact that he had effectively retired in 1865, shortly after the death of his wife, Margaret Barnhill Roosevelt, on January 23, 1861.

Among the collections of the Oyster Bay Historical Society is the logbook of the *D.R. Martin*, one of the steamboats that made daily runs from the wharf at the end of Steamboat Landing Road. An entry dated September 27, 1867, states that the *D.R. Martin* shipped a piano, a box, a wheelchair, a commode and a camp stool from Oyster Bay to the Union Dock in New York City for an unnamed Roosevelt. The *Doctor Martin*, as the ship was

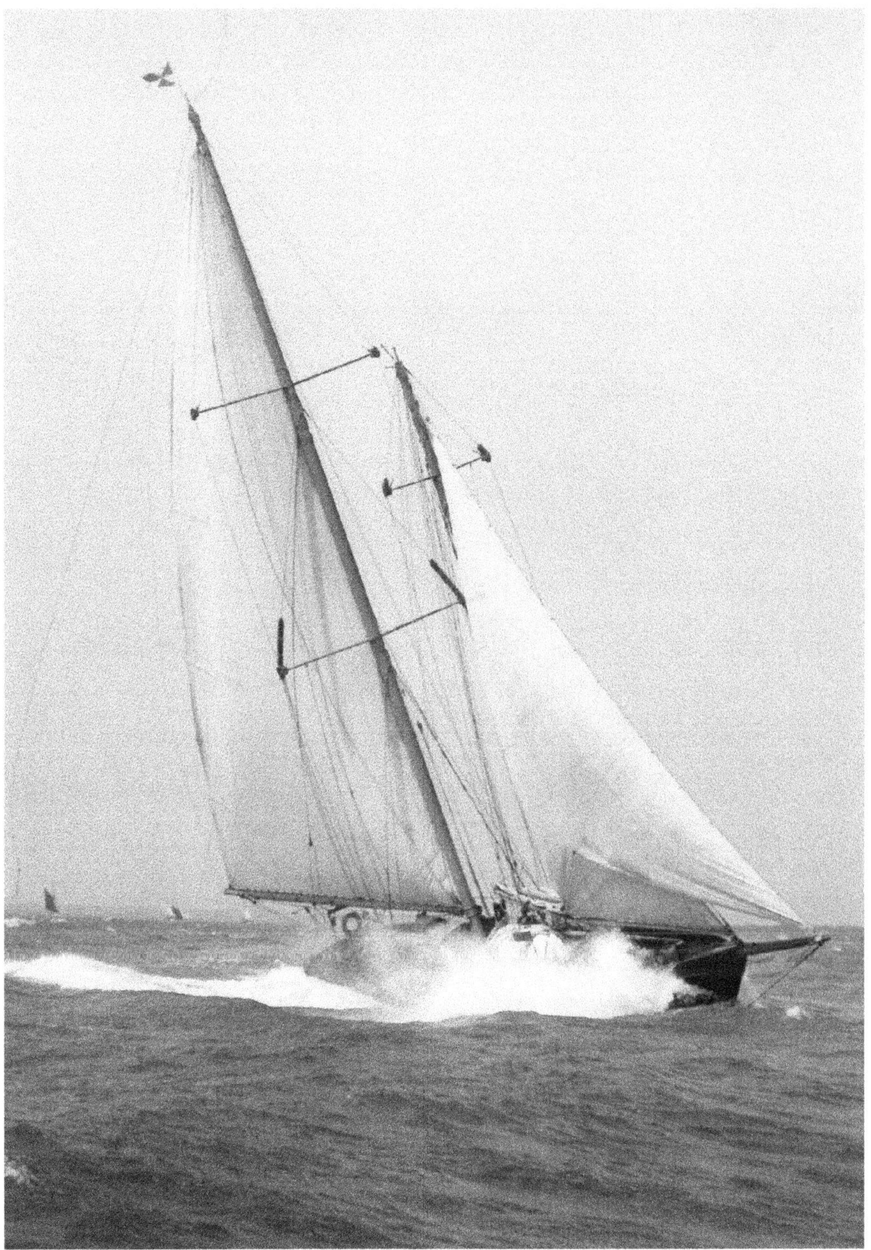

George E. Roosevelt's *Mistress* was a keen competitor in the Seawanhaka Yacht Club races. *Courtesy of the Oyster Bay Historical Society.*

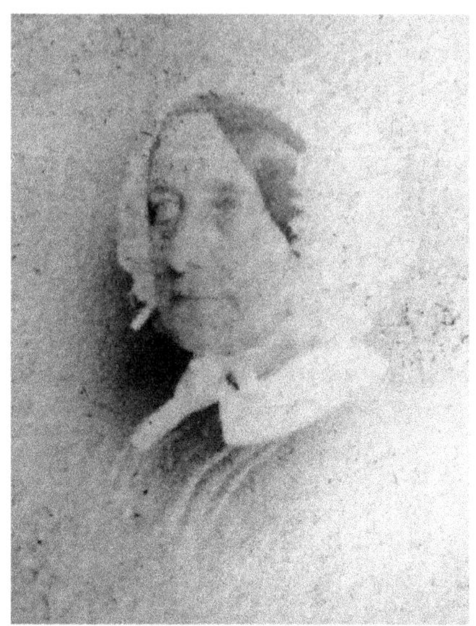

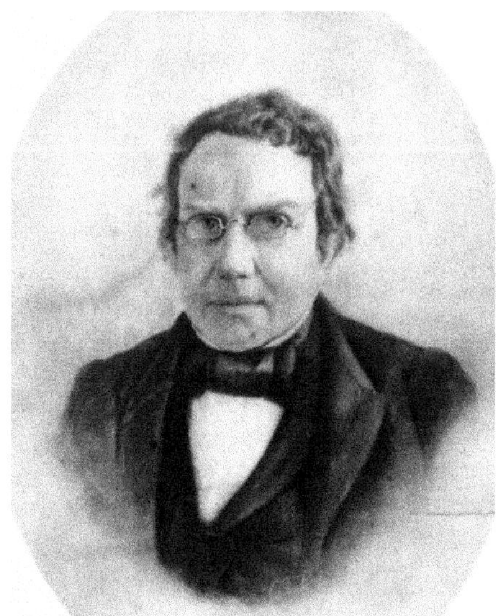

Left: Margaret Barnhill was the wife of CVS Roosevelt and the grandmother of Theodore Roosevelt. She died in 1861. *Courtesy of the Roosevelt family.*

Right: Cornelius Van Schaack Roosevelt was the grandfather of Theodore Roosevelt. He died in Oyster Bay in 1871. *Courtesy of the Roosevelt family.*

called by the boys around the New York Harbor, was a large paddle steamer with large hog frames on each side to stiffen its structure. The boat made daily trips, leaving Oyster Bay at eight o'clock each morning and arriving at the East River pier about three hours later before repeating the trip in the evening. Many years later, the *D.R. Martin* was chartered by Seawanhaka Corinthian Yacht Club for the usage of the race committee and to take guests out to view the races during their regattas.

Silas Weir Roosevelt was born in New York City on October 18, 1823. He was the oldest of Cornelius Van Schaack Roosevelt's and his wife, Margaret Barnhill's, six sons. Silas graduated from Colombia College and became a lawyer who was well-grounded in the profession. He married Mary West in Philadelphia on October 23, 1845, and they had five sons: Cornelius, Hilborne, James West, Frank and an unnamed son that died in childbirth. For many years, Silas practiced law with a great deal of success, and in the 1850s, he was elected as a commissioner for the Public Schools of New York City and as a member of the New York City Board of Education. This was a major turning point in his life, as he began neglecting his law practice and devoted his efforts to the cause of public education.

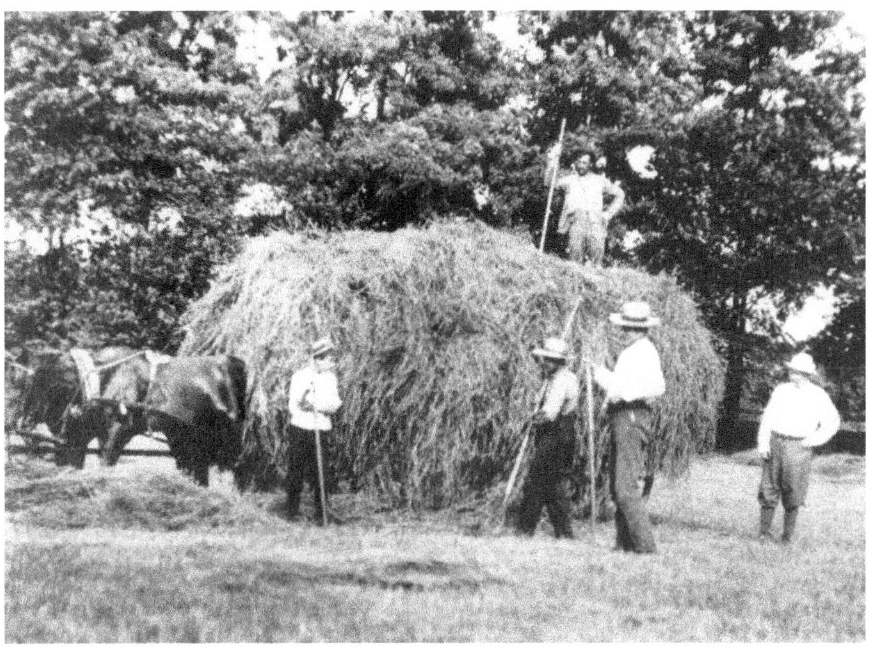

Theodore Roosevelt *(farthest to the right)* observes some of his estate workers at *Sagamore Hill. Courtesy Sagamore Hill National Historical Site.*

Even after being crippled by disease, which ultimately claimed his life, he continued attending school visitations and supporting public education. Silas Weir Roosevelt wrote a book of poetry titled *Kaatskill,* which was published posthumously in December 1870. In the introduction to that small volume, James W. Gerard wrote about Silas: "We all knew of his varied scientific and literary acquirements, there were but few of us who were aware that he had the soul of poetry within him. These fugitive pieces, however, written from boyhood to his latter days, show an exquisite taste and sensibility, and the cultivation of every sentiment that is refined in our nature."

The commode and wheelchair listed on the *D.R. Martin* were used by Silas Weir Roosevelt during the last years of his illness, which had left him paralyzed. He died on March 24, 1870, at just forty-six years old. His son, Cornelius, was among the founding signers of the charter for the Seawanhaka Corinthian Yacht Club on December 30, 1871. Cornelius and his brother, Hilborne, operated a steam yacht named the *Fearless.* They also had a twenty-three-foot catboat named the *Ona-Way.*

WALDECK

James West Roosevelt, son of Silas Weir Roosevelt, was born on July 2, 1858, in New York City. He was just eleven years old when his father died, which was perhaps his inspiration to enter the medical profession. James graduated from the College of Physicians and Surgeons in 1880 and served on the staff of Roosevelt Hospital. Dr. Roosevelt married Laura Henriette d'Oremieulx in New York City on February 26, 1884. The couple lived in New York City, but they also had a summer home in Cove Neck on four acres of land called *Waldeck*, which overlooked Oyster Bay Harbor, just to the north of *Yellowbanks*. Dr. Roosevelt died at his 32 East Thirty-First Street, New York City home on April 10, 1896, from pneumonia he had contracted only a few days earlier. His sudden death took the family by surprise. His widow, Laura d'Oremieulx, became the founding president of the North Shore Garden Club in 1913, and she continued to live at the family home until her death in 1945.

HILLSIDE

Cornelius Van Schaack rented a home from Richard Irvin, the grandfather of Frances Irvin, author of *Oyster Bay: A Sketch*, on East Main Street, Oyster Bay, known as *Hillside*. Richard Irvin was born in Glasgow, Scotland, in 1799 and came to America in 1823, joining his uncle, Thomas Irvin, in the shipping business. Francis Irvin wrote, "My grandfather, Richard Irvin, bought the place in 1860," but William Peck recorded that the purchase actually took place 1861 when Richard Irvin bought two acres for $7,000 from William H. Bridgens and his wife, Elithere. Peck further notes that he leased the house for several summers to James A. Roosevelt. Richard Irvin died at *Hillside* in June 1888.

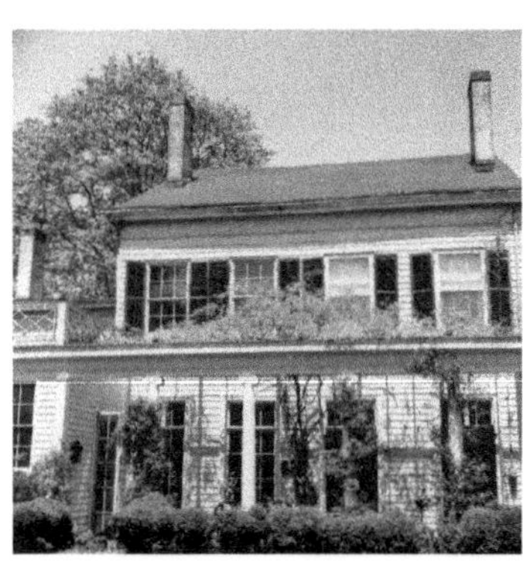

CVS Roosevelt was the first Roosevelt in Oyster Bay. He rented *Hillside* on East Main Street from the Irvin family. *Courtesy John Hammond.*

Yellowbanks

On November 19, 1880, James Alfred Roosevelt bought eighty acres of land in Cove Neck from Daniel Kelsey Youngs for $250 an acre. This was the first time any Roosevelt had purchased land in Oyster Bay. In 1881, on this land, James A. proceeded to build a large Victorian shingle-style home designed by architect Bruce Price, which he named *Yellowbanks* after the large sand banks that led toward Oyster Bay Harbor. Corinne Roosevelt Robinson wrote in her book *My Brother Theodore Roosevelt*, "One of our greatest delights was to take the small rowboats with which we were provided and row away for long days of happy leisure to what then seemed a somewhat distant spot on the other side of the bay, called *Yellow Banks* [*sic*], where we would have our picnic lunch and climb Cooper's Bluff."

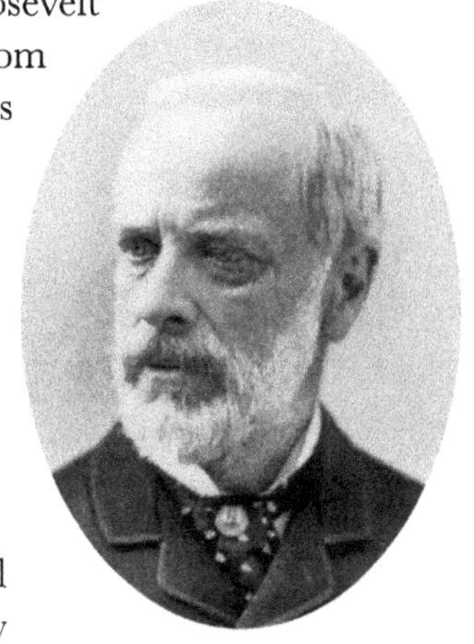

James Alfred Roosevelt was the first Roosevelt to purchase land at Oyster Bay in 1880. James died on his way home to Oyster Bay in 1898 on a Long Island Railroad train somewhere around Mineola. *Courtesy of the Oyster Bay Historical Society.*

In the days before electricity, keeping things cold with refrigeration was difficult. James A. Roosevelt solved the problem by constructing two ice ponds on land at the lowest point of his property. The ponds were filled with fresh water during the summer months, which would freeze during the winter season, forming thick ice. The ice was then harvested and transported to his icehouse, where it was covered with straw to keep it cool. This method of making ice was used from the 1880s to the 1920s to provide ice throughout the summer. James's ice ponds survive on the west side of Cove Neck Road, shortly before the entrance to *Sagamore Hill*. Many years ago, the integrity of the ponds was compromised, and the resulting breach now allows salt water to penetrate them.

James Alfred Roosevelt was born on June 13, 1825, in New York City. He was the son of Cornelius Van Schaack Roosevelt and a brother of Theodore Roosevelt Sr. James A. joined the mercantile firm of his father when he was twenty years old, and, at age forty-five, he took over the operations of the firm when his father retired in 1865. He was also the vice president of the Chemical Bank of New York as well as the Broadway Improvement Company. He married Elizabeth Norris Emlen on December 22, 1847.

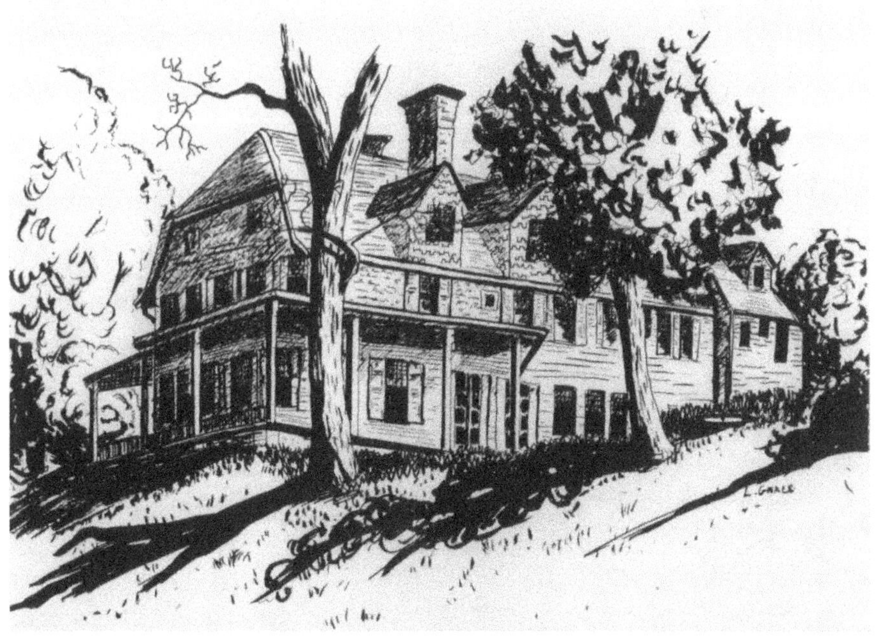

Yellowbanks was built by James A. Roosevelt in 1881 on land bought from the Youngs family. It was passed through inheritance to his only surviving son, William Emlen Roosevelt, in 1912, and, then, in 1936, to John Kean Roosevelt, the father of Elizabeth Roosevelt, the coauthor of this book. Drawn by Lorraine Grace for the publication *Walls Have Tongues*. *Courtesy of the Oyster Bay Historical Society.*

During the Civil War, James A. Roosevelt organized considerable civilian support for the Union cause through his efforts in the United States Sanitary Commission and the Western Sanitary Commission. Through these organizations, James A. raised funds to provide clothing and medical care to Union soldiers on the field. James A. was the financial advisor to many members of his family. Theodore Roosevelt wrote to Edith Carow, in 1880, that he was "in frightful disgrace with Uncle Jim on account of [his] expenditures, which certainly [had] been heavy." James A. Roosevelt died on July 15, 1898, somewhere around Mineola while aboard a Long Island Railroad train bound for Oyster Bay. When the train arrived at the Oyster Bay station, James was found dead in his seat.

After the death of James A. Roosevelt, his widow, Elizabeth Norris Emlen Roosevelt, lived at *Yellowbanks* until her death on January 26, 1912. At that time, the home was passed down to their only surviving son, William Emlen Roosevelt; they had another son, Alfred Roosevelt, born on April

2, 1856, but he had been killed in a railroad accident in Mamaroneck, New York, on July 3, 1891. On January 10, 1893, Elizabeth A. Roosevelt donated bonds in the amount of $1,500 to the Seawanhaka Yacht Club in memory of her son, Alfred. The money was to be used as a memorial to him in the form of a sailing prize, which has come to be known as the Alfred Roosevelt Cup and is still a treasured sailing prize at Seawanhaka.

William Emlen Roosevelt, known by his middle name, Emlen, was born on April 30, 1857, in New York City. He married Christine Griffin Kean in Elizabeth, New Jersey, on October 4, 1883. Emlen and his wife, Christine, had five children, who were raised at *Yellowbanks* and in New York City: Christine Kean, born on August 3, 1884; George Emlen, born on October 13, 1887; Lucy Margaret, born on November 7, 1888; John Kean, born on September 22, 1890; and Philip James, born on May 22, 1892. Emlen was a prominent New York City banker and took over most of the financial positions previously held by his father. He was a director and officer in several firms, the head of Roosevelt & Son and the president of Roosevelt Hospital. Emlen was the first cousin of Theodore Roosevelt and his best friend. In the fall of 1878, Emlen and Theodore, along with their cousin James West Roosevelt, embarked on a hunting expedition to the woods of Penobscot County, Maine. Their guides on this expedition were William Wingate Sewall and his nephew, Wilmot Dow. Two years later, from August 16 to September 7, 1880, Emlen engaged the same guides for a second hunting and fishing trip to the same area. Emlen's cousin Theodore had made good use the guides a few years later by hiring them to run his ranches in the Badlands. Emlen loved sailing and was a very active member of Seawanhaka Corinthian Yacht Club on Centre Island. All of the Roosevelt males who lived on Cove Neck were very active members. Theodore Roosevelt was not an active sailor; he preferred rowboats.

After the death of Theodore in 1919, Emlen bought up the remaining plots in Youngs Memorial Cemetery to be saved for future generations of Roosevelts. He also bought the additional acres for the Theodore Roosevelt Bird Sanctuary. However, when Emlen died on March 15, 1930, he did not use one of those plots at Youngs. Instead, he was buried at the Greenwood Cemetery in Brooklyn, where many prior generations of Roosevelts had also been buried. His widow, Christine Griffin Kean Roosevelt, died on February 29, 1936, and was also buried at Greenwood. John Kean Roosevelt was the middle son of Emlen Roosevelt and was born in Elizabeth, New Jersey. He married Elise Annette Weinacht at Trinity Church on September 22, 1916. John Kean Roosevelt became a partner in Roosevelt & Son and lived in Glen Cove until 1936, when he inherited *Yellowbanks* upon the death of his mother. John Kean Roosevelt and Elise Annette Weinacht were the parents of Elizabeth Emlen Roosevelt, the coauthor of this history.

The *Yellowbanks* home required a large staff of servants to keep it running. The 1900 U.S. Census was taken at the estate on June 16, 1900, and lists the various servants at *Yellowbanks*. There were two kitchen maids, two parlor maids, one cook, a butler and his assistant, two coachmen, two grooms, three gardeners and a boat captain. Most of the staff would return with the family to the city each fall, but the gardeners, grooms and boat captain remained at *Yellowbanks* year-round.

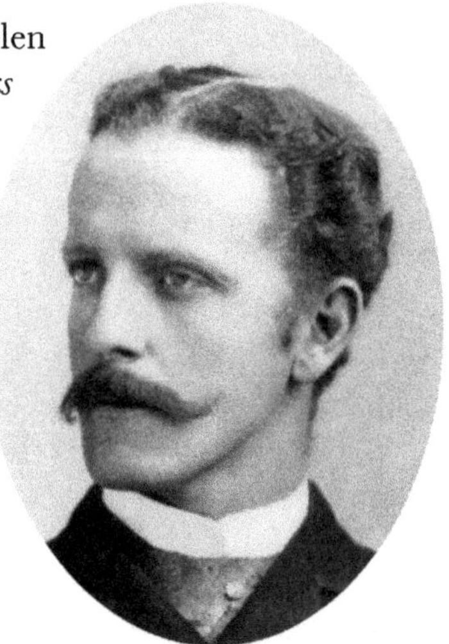

Emlen Roosevelt was a son of James A. Roosevelt and the first cousin and best friend of Theodore Roosevelt. *Courtesy of the Oyster Bay Historical Society.*

ELFLAND

Leila Roosevelt was born in New York City on February 5, 1850. She was a daughter of James A. Roosevelt and Elizabeth Norris Emlen. Leila married Montgomery Roosevelt Schuyler on February 21, 1870. They eventually divorced, and she married her second husband, Edward Reeve Merritt, on April 26, 1890. Divorce was frowned upon by the Roosevelts at that time, and because of that, the Merritts suffered some degree of exclusion by Leila's family members. The Merritts lived on a property known as *Elfland* on the south side of the present entrance road to *Sagamore Hill*. The home was built around 1900 and was torn down in the 1930s. Leila Roosevelt Merritt died in Oyster Bay on September 18, 1934, and Edward Reeve Merritt died on February 22, 1931.

Gracewood

George Emlen Roosevelt was the eldest son of William Emlen Roosevelt and Christine Griffin Kean, and he was born on October 13, 1887. George graduated from Harvard in 1909 and soon became a partner in Roosevelt & Son. He was also an active member of Seawanhaka Yacht Club and eventually acquired a new black-hulled sailing yacht, which he named the *Mistress*. His brother John Kean Roosevelt tried to send a telegram to him congratulating him, but the Western Union office refused to send the telegram, which said, "Congratulations on your Black Mistress." George Emlen served as a lieutenant colonel during the First World War. On October 24, 1914, he married Julia Morris Addison at St. John's Church in Stamford, Connecticut. After their marriage, the couple moved into *Gracewood*, the former home of James King Gracie. George's father, Emlen, had acquired the home after the death of Gracie in 1903.

James King Gracie was born in 1840 in Savannah, Georgia, and married Anna Bulloch, the sister of Theodore Roosevelt's mother, Martha Bulloch. Anna was the daughter of James Stephen Bulloch and Martha Stewart Bulloch and was born in Savannah, Georgia, on September 15, 1833. James King Gracie was from an old family that once owned Gracie Mansion, the historic home of New York City's mayor. In the summer of 1877, the Gracies were living in an old farmhouse in Whitestone, near Flushing. Theodore Roosevelt and his brother, Elliott, rowed over to visit them. A couple of years later, Gracie bought property at Cove Neck and built *Gracewood*. At the same time, Theodore Roosevelt was building *Sagamore Hill*, and *Yellowbanks* was being built by James Alfred Roosevelt.

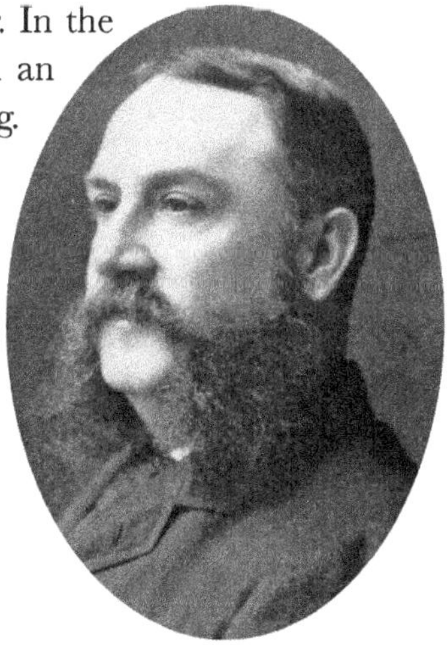

James K. Gracie was the husband of Anna Bulloch. He purchased property on Cove Neck and built *Gracewood* around 1885. *Courtesy of the Oyster Bay Historical Society.*

Gracewood was designed by McKim, Mead & White and had a well at the bottom of the hill. Water from the well was pumped up to *Gracewood* via windmill. From there, the water was fed, by gravity, down the hill to *Yellowbanks*, providing the estate with water on its first two floors. Elizabeth Roosevelt recalled, "The water from the well did not run to the third floor, where the servants lived. It only went up as far as the second at the *Yellowbanks* house. You had to carry the water up to the third floor." Two-year-old Eleanor Roosevelt, the daughter of Theodore Roosevelt's brother, Elliott, spent about six months of 1886 living with her great-aunt Anna Bullock and great-uncle James K. Gracie at *Gracewood* while her own parents sailed to Europe. Young Eleanor became closely acquainted with her first cousin Alice Roosevelt during this stay. Anna Bullock Gracie died in Oyster Bay on June 9, 1893, at the age of fifty-nine. She was buried in Greenwood Cemetery in Brooklyn.

Dolonor

Philip James Roosevelt Sr., the youngest son of Emlen Roosevelt, was born on May 15, 1892. He graduated Harvard in 1913 and served as a captain in the First World War with the American Expeditionary Forces. For his bravery during his service, he was awarded the Croix de Guerre. He became a partner in Roosevelt & Son and a director of several corporations, as well as a commodore of Seawanhaka Yacht Club. Philip Roosevelt was an accomplished sailor and had won the Alfred Roosevelt Memorial Cup, named in honor of his uncle Alfred Roosevelt, at Seawanhaka Yacht Club when he was only eleven years old.

In 1919, Philip Roosevelt became the president of a joint venture that involved several of his Roosevelt cousins. His cousin Kermit had gone with his father, Theodore, on a South American expedition, where he became intrigued by the South American coffeehouses. With the passage of the Eighteenth Amendment (Prohibition) on January 29, 1919, Kermit believed that coffeehouses could be a satisfactory substitution for bars as gathering places. He pitched the idea to Philip James Roosevelt, Theodore Roosevelt Jr., Archibald Roosevelt, Ethel Roosevelt Derby and her husband, Dr. Richard Derby. The group formed a corporation and opened the Brazilian Coffee House on West Forty-Fourth Street, Manhattan, in 1919. They later changed the name to the R & R Coffee House, which remained in operation until 1928, when it was sold. On May 9, 1925, Philip James married his second cousin and the daughter of John Ellis Roosevelt, Jean Schermerhorn Roosevelt, in Glen Head, New York.

Philip James Roosevelt was given property adjoining *Sagamore Hill* as a wedding gift from his father, William Emlen Roosevelt, in 1925. Philip and Jean spent their honeymoon touring China and Mongolia, where they were captivated by the Chinese art. When they returned, they commissioned Hall Pleasants Pennington, an architect, to build *Dolonor*, their home. It was named after the Chinese trade city of the same name and was completed in 1928. They raised three children at *Dolonor*: Philippa, Philip James and John E. Roosevelt.

On the afternoon of November 8, 1941, Philip Roosevelt had just finished lunch with his family and tuned on the radio to listen to some football games when he decided, around 3:30 in the afternoon, to go down to his dock on Cold Spring Harbor and take a sail in a small sailboat, which some reports say was a dingy. About an hour later, his wife went down to check on him and found him dead in his car. The small sailboat had capsized and forced Philip to swim to shore in the frigid November water. Dr. Richard Derby, husband of Ethel Roosevelt Derby, said that he had died from overexertion and the shock of the cold water while swimming to shore.

Tranquility

Theodore Roosevelt Sr. brought his family, for several summers, to the summer home of his father, Cornelius. On August 1, 1870, eleven-year-old Theodore Roosevelt entered into his diary, "Was sick so went to Oyster Bay by boat cars and coach"; the term "cars" refers to railcars. A month later, he wrote that he had lost his diary until September 10, when he wrote that he had been at Oyster Bay and Richfield during the month of August. Theodore Roosevelt Sr. began renting a home on Cove Road, which came to be named *Tranquility* by the family, and Theodore's sister Corinne recalled many years later, "Anything less tranquil than that happy home at Oyster Bay can hardly be imagined."

Theodore's father had been searching for a home he could afford to rent for the summers; he had rented homes in Richfield, New York, and at Dobbs Ferry, New York, before coming to Oyster Bay. After the death of his own father, Cornelius, in 1871, he finally had the resources, but before he rented his home in Oyster Bay, he took his family on a grand tour of Europe and Egypt. For the entirety of the summer of 1874, Theodore Roosevelt Sr. rented *Tranquility* from Smith Thompson Van Buren, the son of President Martin Van Buren. Many biographers have erroneously attributed the ownership of the house to the Swan family due to Otis Swan's rental of the home before Theodore Roosevelt. When the Beers, Comstock and Kline

Company published its book *Queens County Atlas* in 1873, it listed Otis Swan as the resident of the property, but Swan vacated the property and left his furnishings, which were later used by the Roosevelt family.

Theodore Roosevelt Sr. may have learned about *Tranquility*'s availability through John Van Buren, another son of Martin Van Buren, or one of the other members of the Union League Club, which included Otis Swan. In her book *My Brother Theodore Roosevelt*, Corinne Roosevelt Robinson wrote, "The summer of 1874 proved to be the forerunner of the happiest summers of our lives, as my father decided to join the colony which had been started by his family at Oyster Bay, Long Island, and we rented a country place which, much to the amusement of our friends, we named *Tranquility*."

In September 1876, Theodore Roosevelt Sr. drove his son Theodore from *Tranquility* to the train depot in Syosset. Young Theodore was about to begin his years at Harvard, and Theodore Roosevelt Sr. was about to take his place as an elected elder of the First Presbyterian Church of Oyster Bay. He was elected at a congregational meeting on July 26, 1877. His term of office began on August 4, 1877, but it was not destined to last very long.

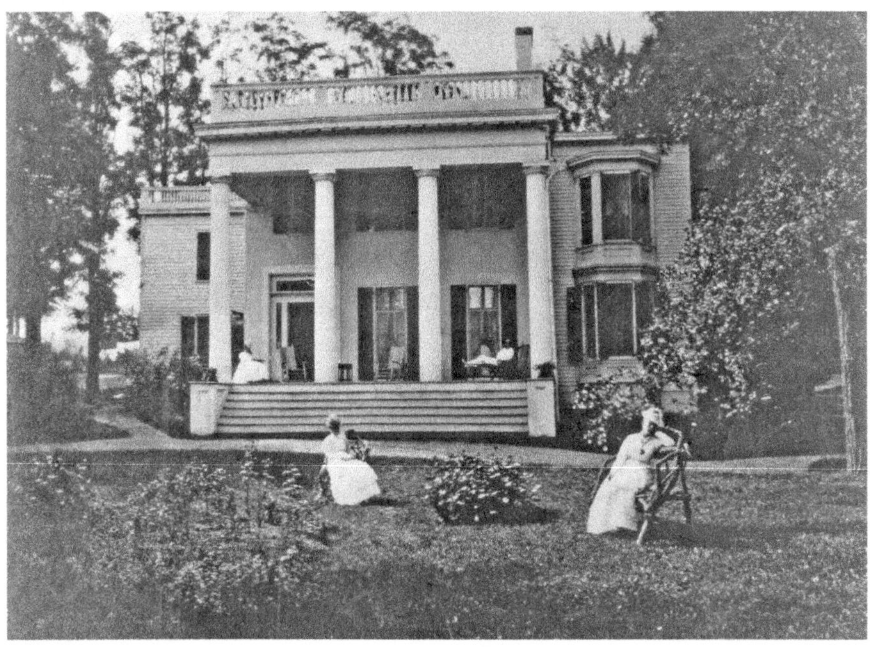

Theodore Roosevelt Sr. rented *Tranquility* from Smith Thompson Van Buren, son of President Martin Van Buren. TR Sr. can be seen in this photo, relaxing on the porch. *Courtesy Sagamore Hill National Historical Site.*

Theodore Roosevelt Sr. died in New York City on February 9, 1878. On his twenty-second birthday, October 27, 1880, Theodore Roosevelt married Alice Hathaway Lee in Brookline, Massachusetts. The couple had to delay their honeymoon, however, as Roosevelt was immersed in his law studies at Columbia. He promised her that, when the time came, they would get away for a real honeymoon. Instead, he took his new bride to *Tranquility* for a week. He wrote his mother, Martha Bullock Roosevelt, about their honeymoon at *Tranquility* on October 31, 1880, "In the afternoon we play tennis or walk in Fleet's woods." Martha Bullock Roosevelt continued to rent *Tranquility* through the summer of 1883 before her death on February 14, 1884.

Sagamore Hill

Shortly after Theodore Roosevelt graduated from Harvard, in 1880, he purchased land in Cove Neck from the Youngs family. The land had been used for grazing the large flocks of Merino sheep that belonged to Daniel Youngs. Roosevelt began planning to build his home, which was to be for himself and his new wife, Alice, and was to be named *Leeholm*. Two weeks after Alice's death, Theodore signed a contract with John A. Wood and Son, carpenters from Lawrence, Long Island, on March 1, 1884, for the construction of *Sagamore Hill*. The contracted price of the home was $16,975, and the architects were Lamb & Rich.

During this time, Theodore supplemented his inheritance by writing articles for various magazines, the most notable being *The Century*. In the April 1885 edition of *The Century*, he wrote a treatise on his experiences in the New York State legislature entitled "Phases of Legislation." The lengthy article told about the many factors that affected the political body and described, in detail, his views on the character of the constituencies of the many legislative districts around the state, including his own in Manhattan. The section in which he wrote about the rural districts got Theodore into trouble with some of his soon-to-be Oyster Bay neighbors.

In describing the rural voters, Roosevelt wrote, "In the country, the constituencies, who are usually composed of honest though narrow-minded and bigoted individuals, generally keep a pretty sharp lookout on their members, and, as already said, the latter are apt to be fairly honest men." In the March 28, 1885 edition of the *East Norwich Enterprise*, the editor advised, "[Theodore Roosevelt's] article ought to be read by everyone and

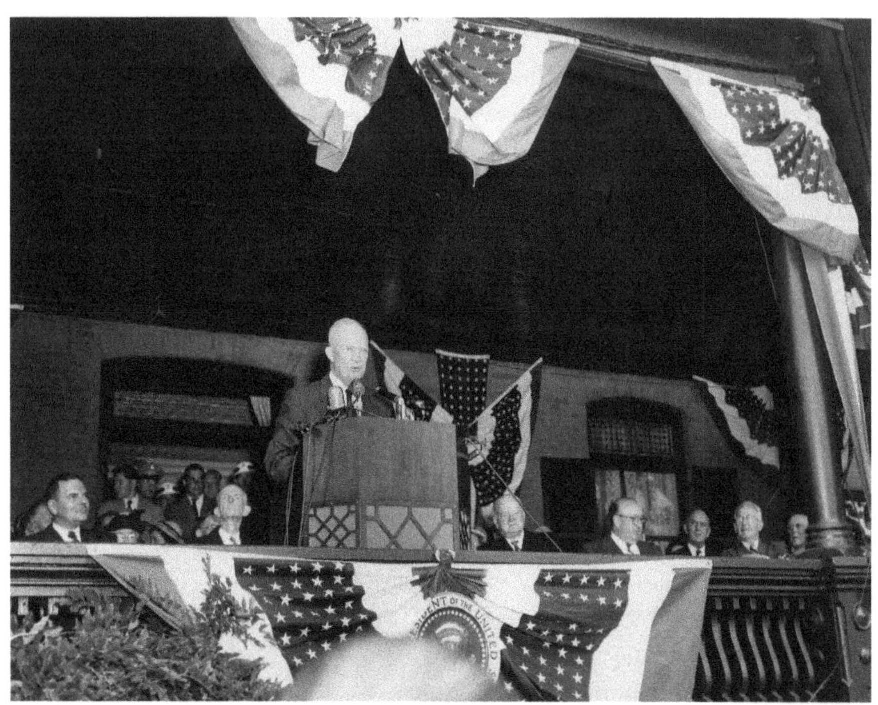

President Eisenhower speaks at the dedication of *Sagamore Hill* in June 1953. To Ike's left is former President Herbert Hoover. *Courtesy of Sagamore Hill National Historical Site.*

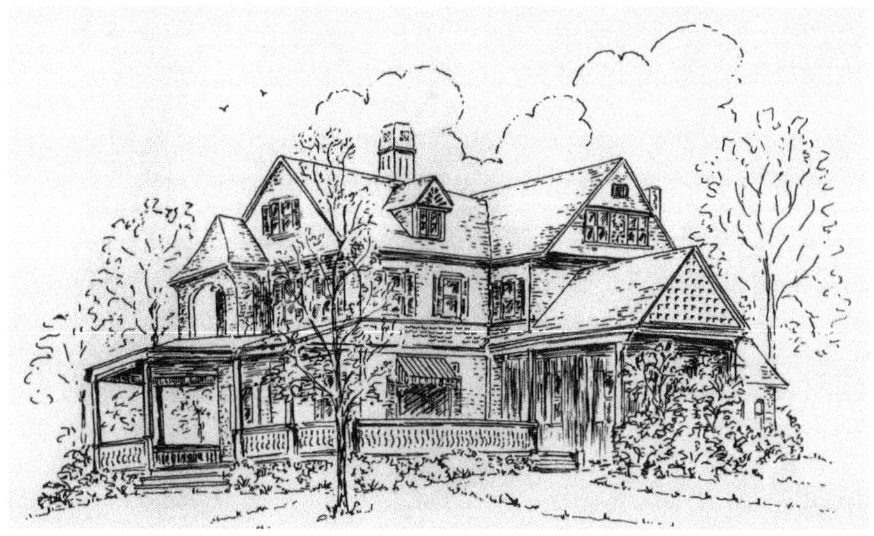

Theodore Roosevelt and his family were the only ones to call *Sagamore Hill* home. This drawing was done by Ruth Armstrong for the publication *Walls Have Tongues. Courtesy Oyster Bay Historical Society.*

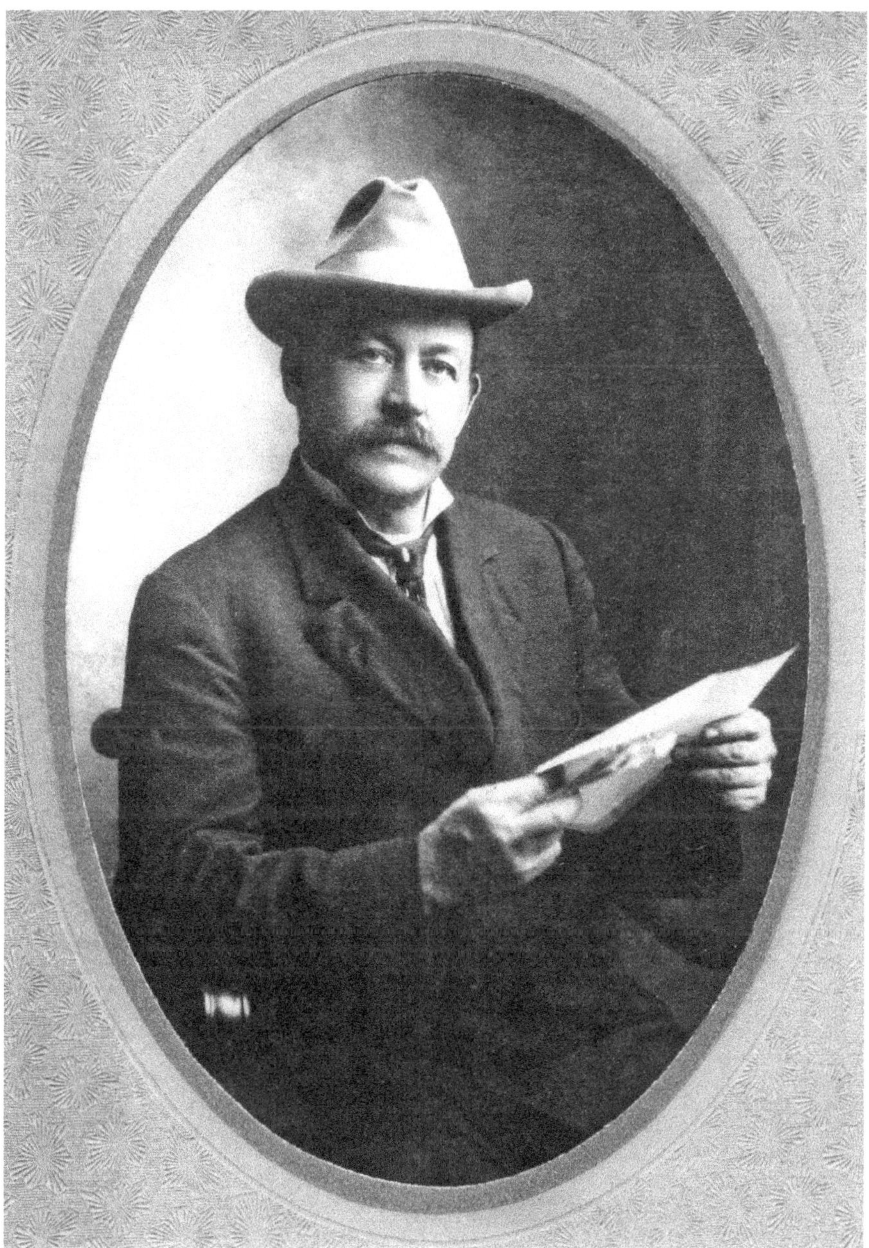

Henry Dollard operated his blacksmith shop on Cove Road and took care of the horseshoeing for many families on Cove Neck. *Courtesy Oyster Bay Historical Society.*

Oyster Bay people for obvious reasons can be justly proud of so valuable a contribution from her gifted citizen." Although the editor of the *Enterprise* was apparently pleased with the article, Roosevelt's comments didn't rest very well with Daniel Kelsey Youngs, whose own son, William Jones Youngs, was a member of the legislature that Roosevelt criticized. Daniel Kelsey Youngs took Theodore to task in a letter to the editor of the *New York Tribune*, dated April 6, 1885. In the letter, Youngs wrote:

> *We of the country take issue with him in his manner of treating country constituencies, which he terms honest, though narrow-minded and bigoted. They were probably loosely from a preconceived, it might almost be said an inherent notion that ignorance and boorishness are necessary characteristics of rural life. To be as plain spoken as he and practice the honesty with which we are credited, we are constrained to say that he has written of that whereof he might be better informed. How can he or any of the class he associates with know anything of country homes.*

Daniel Kelsey Youngs closed his letter with a strong admonition to Roosevelt:

> *Perhaps there would have been less disposition to criticize any of the assertions contained in Mr. Roosevelt's contribution, but the fact that we expect to have him for a near neighbor…and we are unwilling that he should bring with him any erroneous impressions. It is hoped that during his sojourn here that he will become better and more favorably acquainted with country life.…We should like to have Mr. Roosevelt among us as a permanent resident that we may sometime have an opportunity to prove our fitness for political duties and to disprove our narrow-mindedness and bigotry, by adopting him as our representative.*

The words of Daniel Kelsey Youngs did not go unheard. Although it took him some time, Roosevelt did learn the ways of the country people and adopted them wholeheartedly. He even threw off most of the trappings and snobbery of the class in which he was born and raised, but it was several years before Theodore Roosevelt was invited to any social function in the Oyster Bay community. On August 20, 1887, Theodore wrote to his sister Bamie:

> *The male Oysters have had several spasms of sociability recently. Last Saturday, Louis Bell gave a lunch to a dozen of us, to see some tennis. I drove over with Uncle Jimmie Gracie, and walked back with Emlen.*

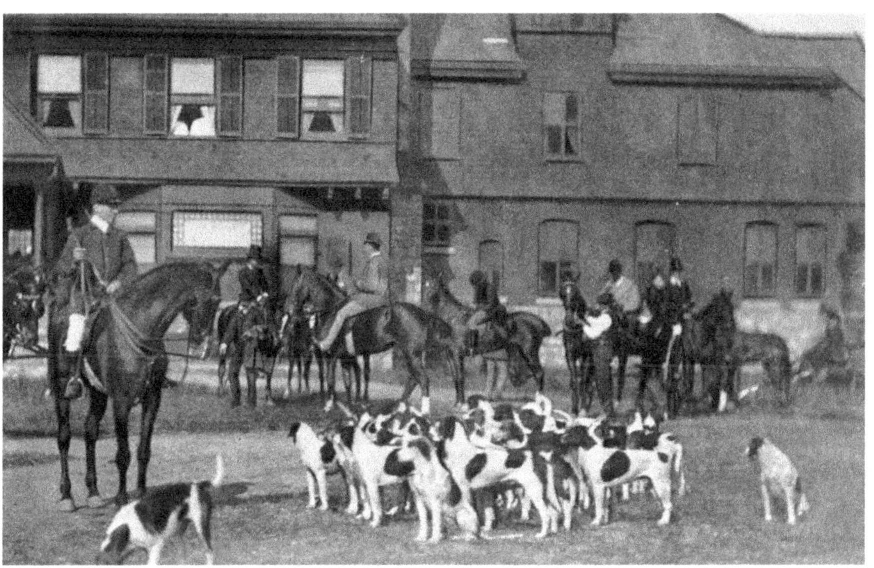

In October 1885, Theodore Roosevelt hosted the Meadowbrook Hunt Club for a fox hunt at *Sagamore Hill. Courtesy of Sagamore Hill National Historical Site.*

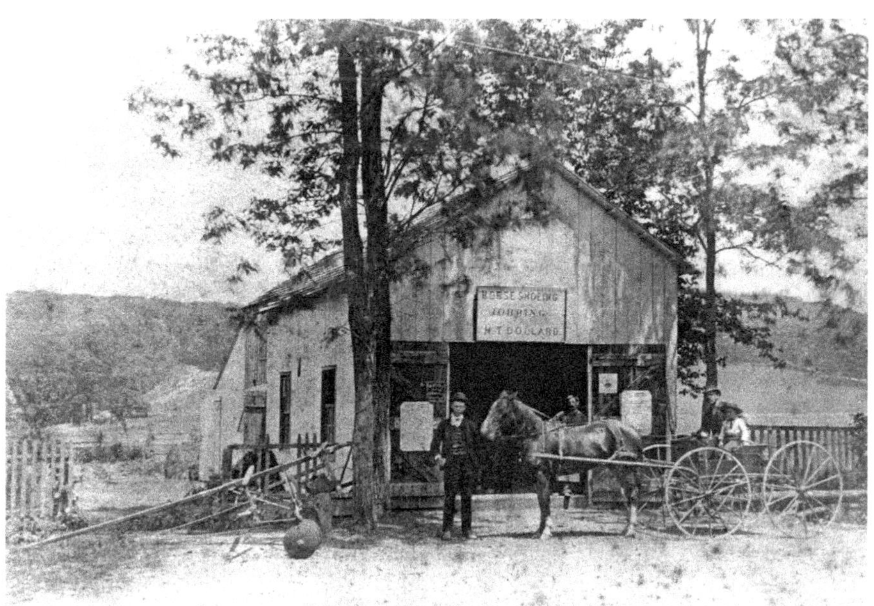

Henry Dollard's blacksmith shop on Cove Road. Dollard built several wagons and carts for Theodore Roosevelt and other residents of Cove Neck. Dollard served on the Oyster Bay School Board. He is buried at Youngs Memorial Cemetery. *Courtesy Oyster Bay Historical Society.*

> *Of all people, Johny Weeks play a match for a hundred and fifty dollars, and lost it! We had great fun, and to day I give a similar lunch, for rifle shooting, tennis etc. We are busily trying to get up a polo club for next year; Emlen is very enthusiastic about it; and I think we will put it through. It will be great fun.*

Within a few years, William Jones Youngs, whose father, Daniel Kelsey Youngs, had previously written the letter admonishing Roosevelt, would become one of Theodore Roosevelt's most trusted advisors.

12
MOHANNES REST CENTER

Kermit Roosevelt, son of President Theodore Roosevelt, was born on October 10, 1889, at *Sagamore Hill.* He married Belle Wyatt Willard on March 11, 1914, at the Chapel of the British Embassy in Madrid, Spain. Belle's father, Joseph Edward Willard, was the ambassador to Spain at the time. Kermit served in both World War I and World War II, and both he and Belle lived at their home in Cove Neck named *Mohannes*, after one of the old Indian sachems. *Mohannes* was a ten-acre estate at the northern tip of Cove Neck that included three hundred feet of shorefront at the entrance to Oyster Bay and Cold Spring Harbor. *Mohannes* was built around 1889 and bought by Kermit Roosevelt and Belle Willard Roosevelt in 1927.

In the early days of World War II, Allied merchant vessels were constantly harassed and sunk by the German U-boat attacks. When ships were attacked, the merchant seamen onboard would suffer from what was described as "convoy fatigue," and they were often unfit to go back to sea. By the summer of 1942, Kermit Roosevelt found himself stationed in Fort Richardson, Alaska, a remote location far from any of the fighting. Kermit and Belle, in an effort to do their part for the war effort, donated *Mohannes* to the War Shipping Administration to be used as a convalescent home for merchant seamen suffering from convoy fatigue.

On September 8, 1942, Eleanor Roosevelt, the wife of President Franklin Roosevelt and first cousin of Kermit Roosevelt, came to Cove Neck to speak at the dedication of the new Seamen's Rest Home. In her remarks, the first lady praised the United Seamen's Service as a very necessary

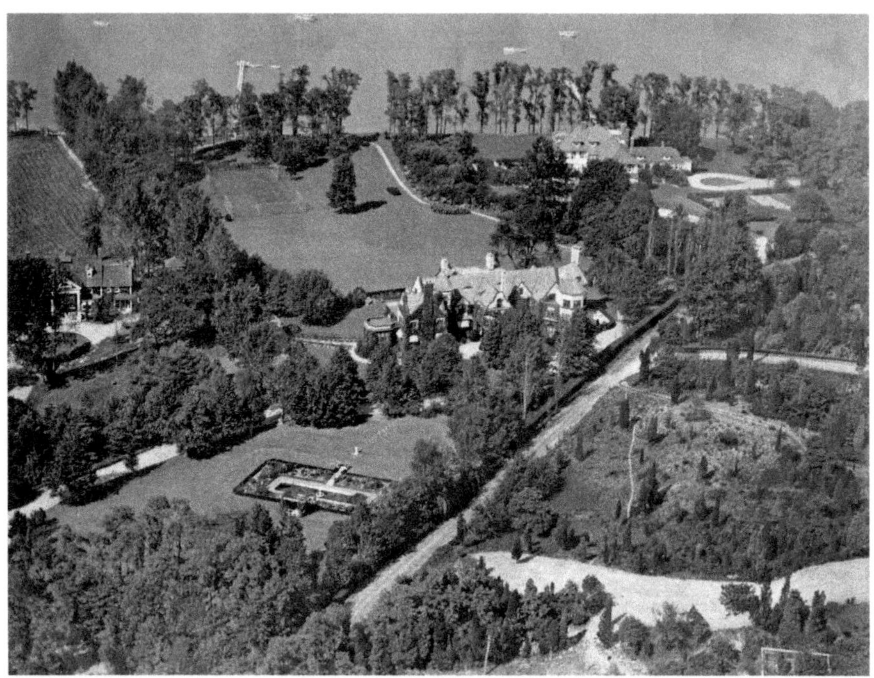

This aerial photo, taken around 1928, shows *Shoredge*, the home of the first mayor of Cove Neck, Howard C. Smith. To the right, and closer to the water, is *Mohannes*, the home of Kermit Roosevelt that became a rest home for merchant mariners during World War II. *Courtesy of The Walker family.*

organization in the war effort, and she told of how the new seamen's rest home would be a wonderful place for the seamen to regain their strength and return to duty. She went on to say that she was "especially glad that it is Major and Mrs. Kermit Roosevelt who [made] this first gesture." Belle Roosevelt was present at the ceremony and turned the keys to the property over to Admiral Emory S. Land of the War Shipping Administration, saying, "It is a joy to welcome the seamen to our home. This is no sacrifice on our part. It is a privilege."

Archie Roosevelt, son of President Theodore Roosevelt and brother of Kermit Roosevelt, was also present at the ceremony but did not choose to speak on the occasion. Archie Roosevelt had been seriously wounded in the First World War and had been declared disabled. At the time of the dedication, Archie was appealing to the War Department to be allowed to join in the fighting of World War II. His appeal was later granted, and he fought in Europe. In his service, he was wounded again and was again classified as disabled. He was the only soldier to be declared disabled in both of the World Wars. Edith Roosevelt, widow of President Theodore Roosevelt, was not able to be present at the dedication due to her failing health and remained at *Sagamore Hill* during the ceremony.

Mohannes was a large twenty-room home that originally had nine bedrooms. A library wing was added in 1927 when Kermit and Belle purchased the, at the time, fifty-year-old house. The library was a large wood-paneled room with high ceilings, two fireplaces and seven windows. There were also several smaller buildings on the estate utilized for the various support functions of the home. After the estate was donated, the barn was turned into a hobby shop where seamen could pursue woodworking, weaving, carving and many other activities. There was also a toy shop where seamen could recondition and repair toys that were later donated to local orphans. Of course, there were also many other activities that the sailors partook in, including ping-pong, chess, checkers and reading a lot of books, magazines and newspapers. Several small sailboats were provided to the seamen to use for recreation and relaxation. Movies were shown regularly in the library, and Broadway stars frequently visited the seamen.

The recovering seamen also had many opportunities to interact with the local community. They made regular trips into Oyster Bay for bowling at DeMartino's bowling lanes in the Trio bar and grill on the corner of Adams Avenue and South Street. Local residents also made frequent trips up to *Mohannes* to visit with the seamen. There were visiting hours all day on Sundays, and visitors could come from one half hour after lunch to one half hour before dinner and from seven o'clock to nine o'clock in the evenings every other day. Among the many local visitors were Beverly (Bev) Baker, who was born in Oyster Bay Cove in 1924, and her close friend, Ann Elizabeth (Betty) Martling, who was born in East Norwich in 1925. Bev and Betty had both graduated from Oyster Bay High School in 1942 and were among the many local youths who went up to *Mohannes* to help brighten the moods of seamen by playing board games, ping-pong or chess with them. Other times, the girls would simply sit and talk, or "shoot the breeze," with them, as they liked to call it.

After three weeks at *Mohannes*, the seamen were evaluated by a medical team to determine whether or not they could return to sea duty. *Mohannes* had a full-time staff of doctors and nurses who were employed by the medical division of the War Shipping Administration. *Mohannes* was extremely successful in its mission, and 78 percent of its patients were returned to active duty after three weeks' convalescence there. The success

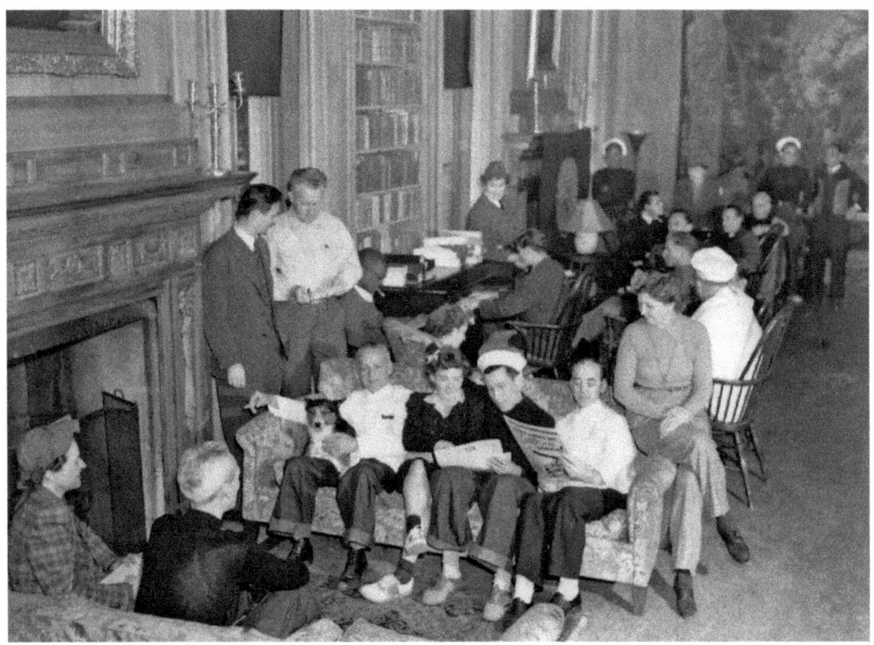

The *Mohannes* Rest Home on the tip of Cove Neck. It was the home of Kermit Roosevelt and was dedicated by First Lady Eleanor Roosevelt as the first rest home for merchant seamen who were victims of Nazi U-boat attacks. *Courtesy Linda Bruder.*

of the *Mohannes* Rest Home in Cove Neck contributed significantly to the war effort and led to the opening of more rest homes in other areas of the country.

Despite all the good he did, Kermit Roosevelt never returned to his home on Cove Neck after the war. On June 4, 1943, he was found dead at Fort Richardson, Alaska. It was determined that his cause of death was a self-inflicted gunshot wound from his own service revolver. He was buried in the U.S. Military Cemetery at Fort Richardson. His widow, Belle Wyatt Willard Roosevelt, also never returned to *Mohannes*; she sold the property in 1945. Belle Wyatt Willard died in New York City on March 30, 1968. *Mohannes* survives today as a private residence.

13
THE LAST ONE LEFT

By Elizabeth Roosevelt

The following story was written by Elizabeth Roosevelt in 2015 for the Oyster Bay Historical Society publication, *The Freeholder*.

In 1881, my great-grandfather James Alfred Roosevelt bought between sixty and seventy acres of land on Cove Neck. He proceeded to have a large Victorian-style house, which he called "Yellow Banks," built on top of a sand bank looking out over Oyster Bay. Across the village road, he built stables for his horses and a tennis court in the woods. There were other buildings built on the property; a cottage for the house keeper, Mrs. Bouts, and in 1927, down by the water, a cottage for the man who took care of the boats, plus a boathouse and a marine railway. When the village incorporated, the large garden area was designated as the business zone.

The family grew and other cousins came to Cove Neck; J. West Roosevelt and his wife took up a small piece of land to the north of "Yellow Banks," Theodore Roosevelt bought the *Sagamore Hill* property. Cousin Leila Merritt built the *Elfland* house on the *Sagamore Hill* Road.

To begin with, these were summer homes, as most of the family worked in New York City and lived in Manhattan in the winter. Summers were busy times for the many cousins, picnicking and rowing, sailing and swimming. A large number of children played together; as they grew up and married, the land was parceled out to them. Theodore Roosevelt's oldest son, Ted, built the house called *Old Orchard*; his brother, Kermit, had a place on the end of the neck.

James Alfred's son, William Emlen, inherited *Yellow Banks* and proceeded to raise three sons and two daughters. His oldest son, George Emlen, bought the *Gracewood* property, which had belonged to the Gracies. Mrs. Gracie was Mrs. Theodore Roosevelt's sister.

William Emlen's youngest son, Philip, was given the land on which he built the *Dolonor* house when he married; then when both William Emlen and his wife died, my father, John Kean Roosevelt, got the *Yellow Banks* property.

Each of these boys proceeded to raise families on Cove Neck. George had two sons and two daughters. They grew up in the late 1920s, and some very wild times were held at *Gracewood*. Only the youngest boy, Julian (Dooley), stayed in the Oyster Bay area after World War II.

Philip James Roosevelt had one daughter and three sons, including Philip James and John E. Roosevelt. When he died in the 1940s, P. James, as he was known, inherited the *Dolonor* property. On his mother's death, that was sold, and he moved to 1 Cove Neck Road. His younger brother and his sister both moved away.

John Kean Roosevelt, in the usual family tradition, had three sons and two daughters. As the boys grew up and married, they moved away, and I alone, of ten girls, continued to live on Cove Neck in the boathouse cottage, now called "The Bilge."

My recollections of Cove Neck really begin with the 1938 hurricane. My older brother, Alfred, was supposed to take me and younger brother, Peter, to the Couderts for a birthday party, but we couldn't get out of the driveway for fallen trees. Surveying the wreckage, the next day was fun for children but lots of work for people working on the estates. We didn't have electricity for several days and trucked water from the artesian well at the bottom of Gracewood Road.

The next event was the coming of World War II. As it got harder to get food items, like butter and meat, my family developed a subsistence farm; we had three cows, some pigs, chickens and a few sheep. My brother, Peter, and I were involved in feeding the chickens, milking the cows and carrying household slops to the pigs. We also did some gardening. There was no time during the war that we weren't fully occupied. We made butter on Saturdays and always took a pound up to cousin Edith at *Sagamore Hill*.

After the war, things began to change. My father sold off the land on the *Sagamore Hill* side of the road. We had less help on what was left; the big garden became a field. Finally, in 1972, I bought the boathouse cottage and, when my cousin P. James died, became the last Roosevelt on Cove Neck.

14

ESTATE WORKERS AND SERVANTS

Prior to the Civil War, Cove Neck consisted of small farms that were operated by a few families. Help on those farms came from occasional farm laborers, who normally worked during harvest time. Daniel Kelsey Youngs employed several farm workers for his extensive properties. In 1853, Edward H. Swan acquired a large holding from the Youngs family and set up his gentleman's farm, and, by 1860, he had six Irish domestic servants working on the property. Swan continued with these six servants through the turn of the twentieth century; however, they were not always the same six, and they were not always Irish.

When the United States Census was taken in February 1920, there were eighty-four residents accounted for in Cove Neck. Only three of the listed residents were property owners: Edith K. Roosevelt, the widow of President Theodore Roosevelt, and William Lincoln Swan and his wife, Belle. The rest of Cove Neck's residents were the estates' servants and their families. Many of the servants also moved to the city each winter, mainly maids and cooks. The servants at *Sagamore Hill*, like Noah Seaman, who was the caretaker that lived in the lodge building, were an exception, as they worked year-round on the property. The family of Charles Henry Griffin was missed in the 1920 Census, since they were living in the Blackton boathouse apartment from 1917 to 1926 and the census taker probably had no knowledge of anyone living there. This was no doubt the problem with other families who were living in quarters on estates.

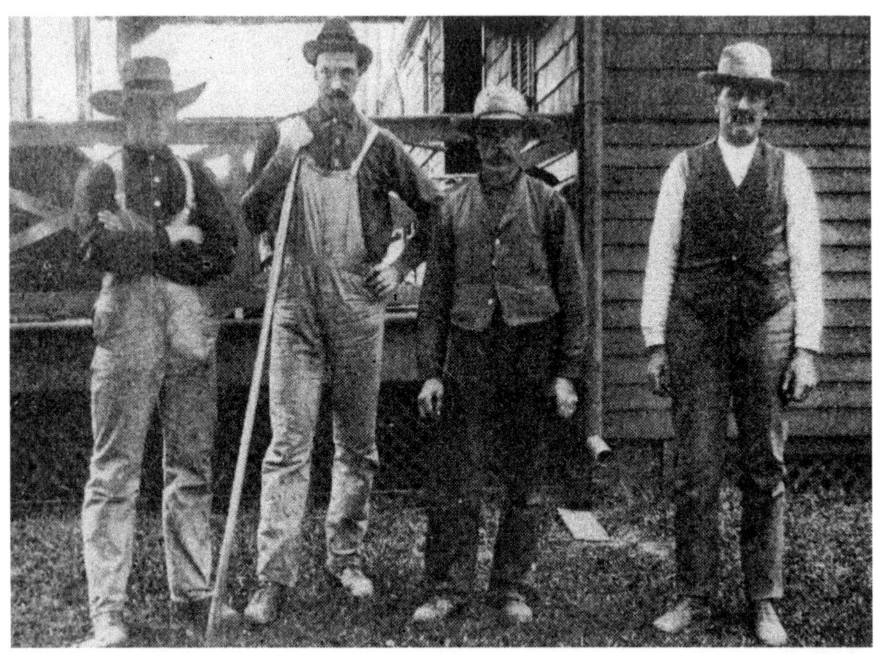

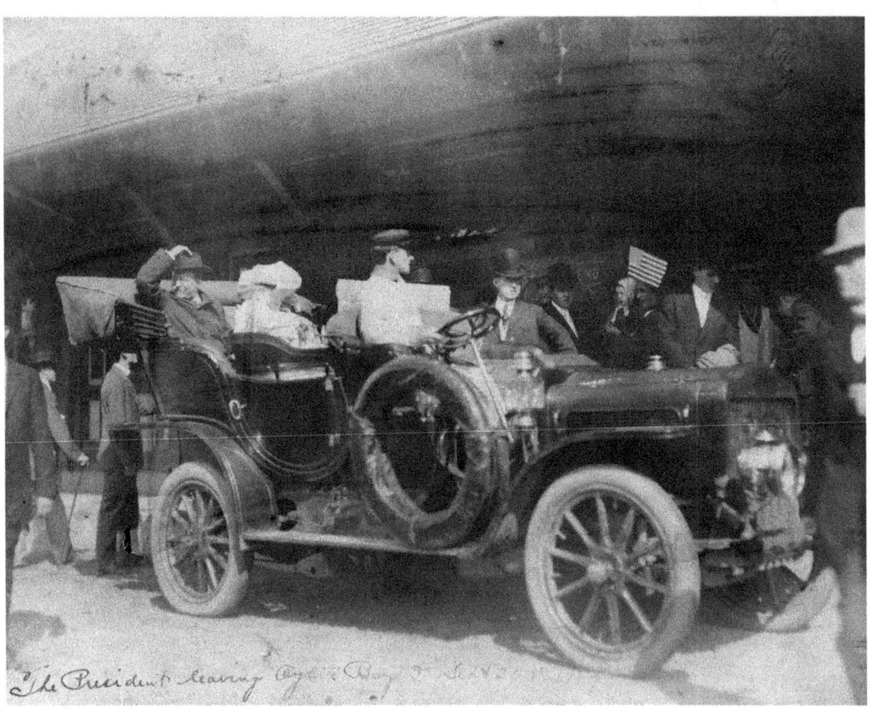
The President leaving

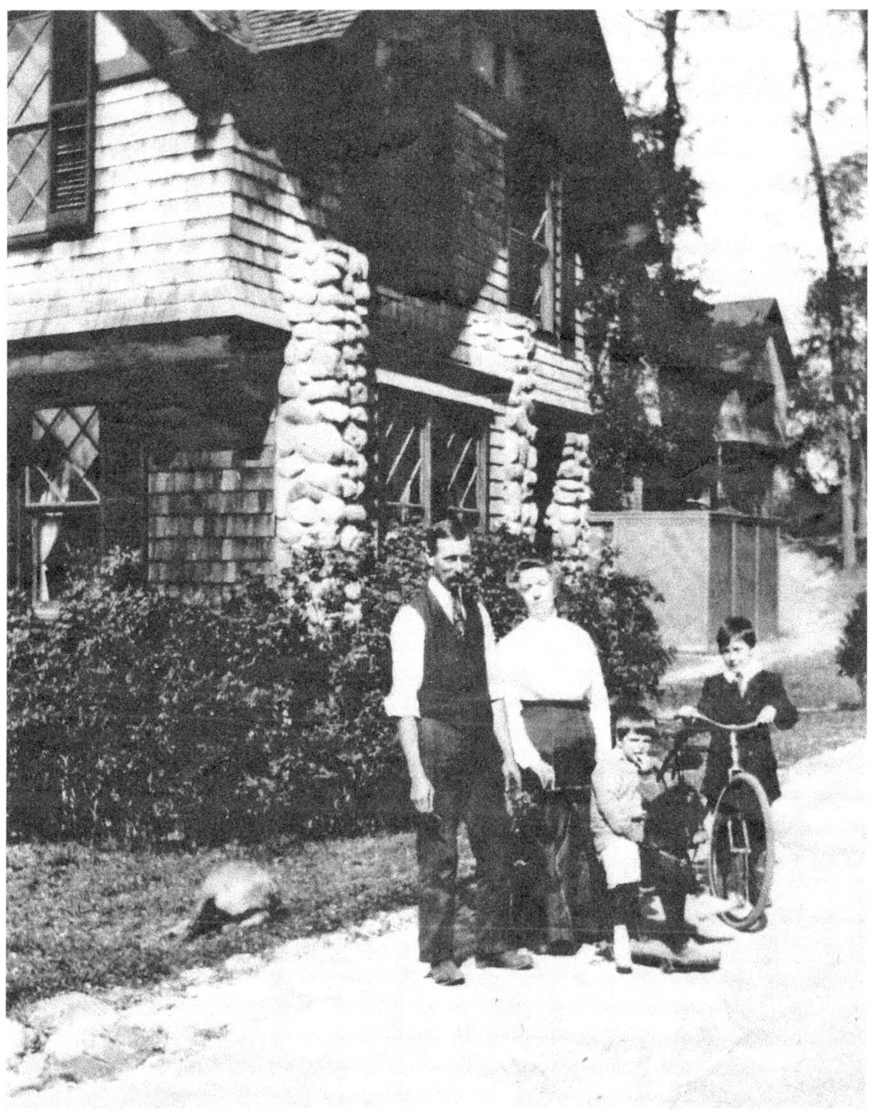

Above: Alfred and Mary Walker with their two boys, Alfred and Daniel, at *Shoredge* cottage. Alfred became a noted commercial artist, and Daniel became the postmaster of Oyster Bay. *Courtesy of the Walker family.*

Opposite, top: Noah Seaman and some of the other estate workers at *Sagamore Hill. Courtesy Sagamore Hill National Historical Site.*

Opposite, bottom: Theodore Roosevelt was the first president to have an automobile. This photo shows him at the Oyster Bay Railroad Station in 1907. The driver is Secret Service agent Herbert Norman Searles, who lived on Simcoe Street in Oyster Bay. *Courtesy of the Theodore Roosevelt Association.*

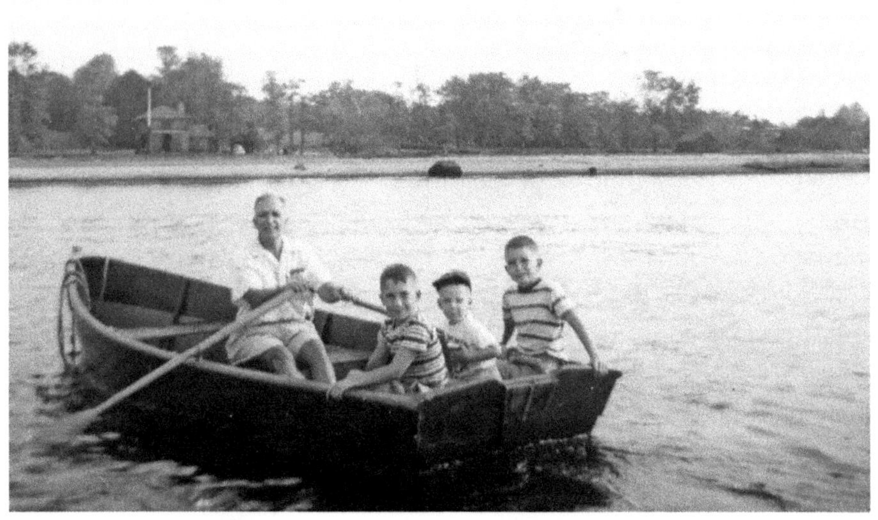

Daniel Walker and his three boys, Daniel, John and Steven. In the background is the boathouse on the Howard C. Smith estate, *Shoredge*. *Courtesy of the Walker family.*

Howard C. Smith, the first mayor of Cove Neck, employed the Walker family at his estate, *Shoredge*. Alfred Walker was born in England and was employed as a gardener and caretaker. His wife, Mary Moloney, was born in Ireland and was employed as a cook. The Walkers had two sons, Alfred, who was born in 1908, and Daniel, who was born around 1904. Both boys attended the Cove School like the other children of the estate workers who lived on Cove Neck.

The Cove School was built in the late 1800s and contained two rooms. It originally included grades one through eight, but after consolidation with the Oyster Bay School District in 1917, only grades one through five were offered. The one schoolroom could be divided into two rooms by a blackboard partition, which could be raised or lowered. Grades one and two were on one side of the room, and grades three, four and five were on the other. Four of the Roosevelt children attended the Cove School during the years that Theodore Roosevelt served as the president of the New York City Police Board: Theodore Roosevelt Jr., Kermit Roosevelt, Ethel Roosevelt and Archibald Roosevelt.

15
INCORPORATION

Howard C. Smith, the first mayor of Cove Neck, wrote to Mrs. William L. Swan in 1929:

> *For a couple of years prior to the close of 1926, there was a good deal of agitation among the residents to find some way to protect us all from the visitations of city automobilists who came in droves and clambered over our properties, picking flowers and shrubs and who left damage in their path. We could get no protection from the Oyster Bay or Nassau County Police and it was finally concluded to draw up a petition for incorporation.*

Mrs. Swan had moved to Baltimore in 1923 with her husband, William Lincoln Swan, to live with her daughter and had, apparently, never been informed of the vote or the incorporation. When the vote was planned, Mr. and Mrs. Theodore Roosevelt Jr. were occupying the old Swan property, and everyone had assumed that they would notify Mrs. Swan. As Smith wrote, "It was felt that the Theodore Roosevelt, Jr.'s, who were in full knowledge of the situation, could keep you posted."

The petition to incorporate was put to a vote of the sixteen property owners who lived in the proposed village. On March 2, 1927, nine of the sixteen property owners who had registered to vote actually voted. The voting was supervised by Charles Ransom, the Oyster Bay town clerk, and was held in the sitting room of the little cottage occupied by Thomas Lake, a gardener for the Howard C. Smith estate, *Shoredge*. Although the last vote

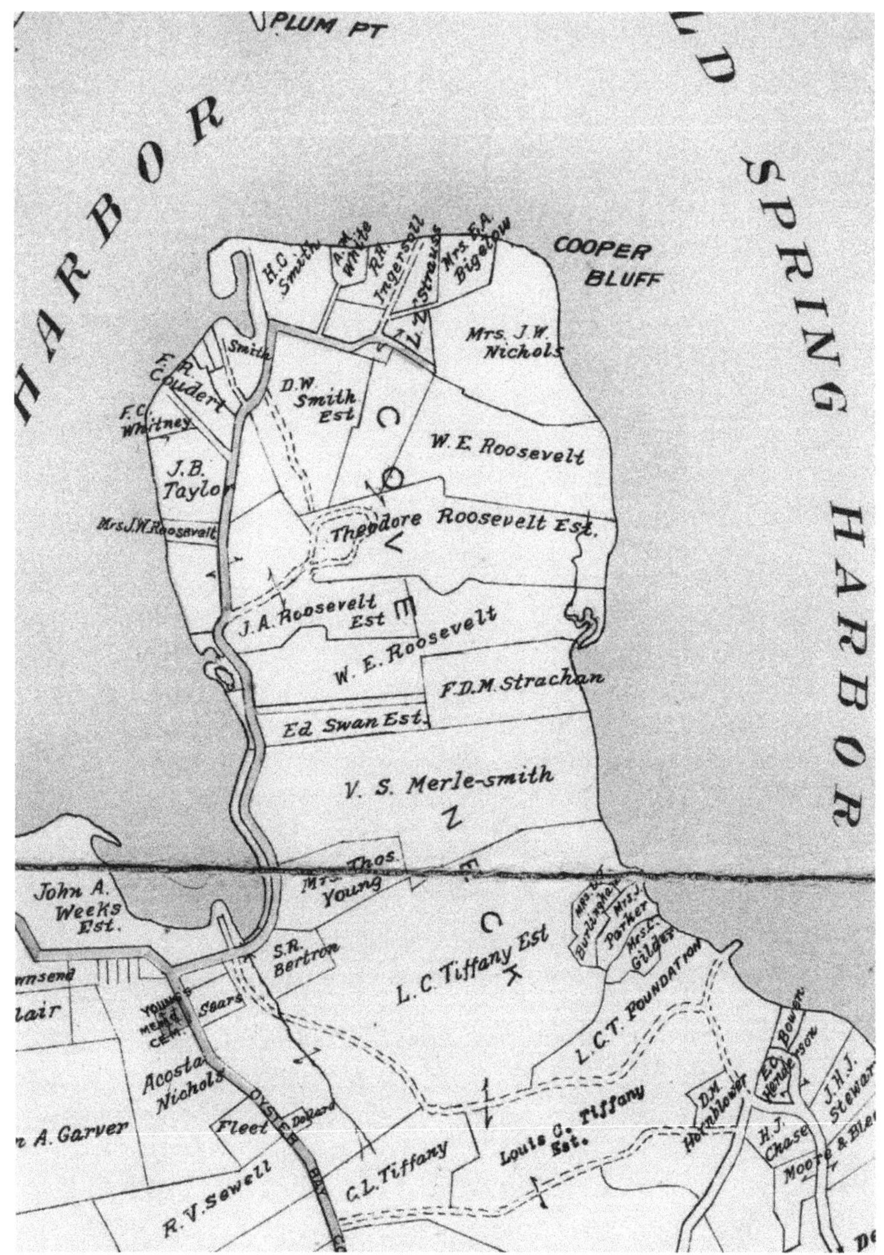

This 1920s vintage map of Cove Neck shows where the various resident voters' properties were located. *Courtesy Oyster Bay Historical Society.*

was cast at about three o'clock in the afternoon, Town Clerk Ransom busied himself reading the latest Booth Tarkington novel while dutifully keeping the polls open until the designated eight o'clock closing hour was reached. The vote was unanimous (9–0) in favor of the petition. A record of the vote, along with other papers relating to the matter, was filed the next day with the town clerk's office by Winslow S. Coates, the attorney of the petitioners. Coates wrote to Howard C. Smith on March 3, 1927, advising him of the outcome of the vote. He said, "Ten days must now elapse before further steps are taken to hold an election of Village officers. The town clerk will, after ten days, appoint a temporary village clerk and three inspectors of election, each of whom must be electors of the territory."

On April 1, 1927, twenty-four voters, three-fifths of the total electorate of the new Incorporated Village of Cove Neck, turned out to Howard C. Smith's garage to cast their ballots for the first village officers. Arriving mostly in limousines, they voted by casting their ballots into a hat. There was no opposition to any of the candidates. James B. Taylor and Alexander White were chosen as trustees, Howard C. Smith was chosen as president (the title later changed to mayor), Mrs. Theodore Roosevelt Jr. was chosen as the treasurer, Alfred M. Mills was chosen as the collector of taxes, Edward Janeway was chosen as the road commissioner and Dr. Raymond A. Lease was chosen as the health commissioner. Immediately following the vote, an organizational meeting was held, and Mrs. Theodore Roosevelt Jr. was appointed as the clerk as well as the treasurer.

Under the New York State Village Law, at that time, a village could not contain more than one square mile of territory, so the southern boundary of the proposed village was set on the southerly side of William Lincoln Swan's property, which is the present-day Tennis Court Road. In 1928, village law was changed by New York State, and additional property owners submitted petitions for their properties to be added to the village. These additional properties included those of Van Santvoord Merle-Smith, the Edward Swan property, the Bertron property and Louis Comfort Tiffany's property. Their petitions were approved, and the boundaries of Cove Neck were established and have remained so to the present day.

One of the first acts of the new village trustees was to hire a policeman. Robert Forest became the first policeman for Cove Neck in 1927, and, in November 1927, he was joined by Frederick Carl. Forest patrolled the streets on a motorcycle and was known to give rides to the children of the village. In September 1931, the strangest event in what would be his lengthy career occurred.

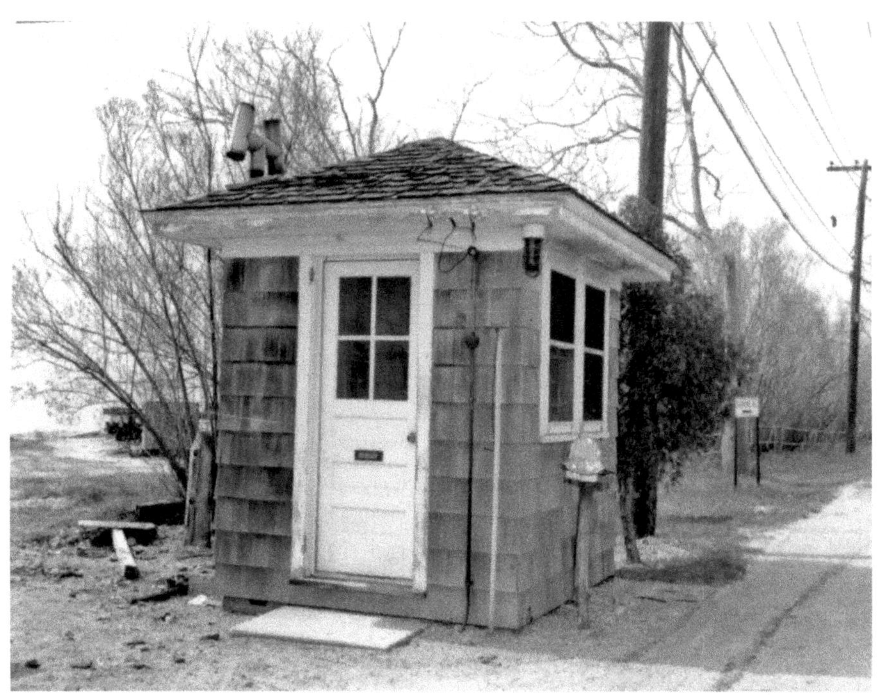

The first police booth was built on land donated to the village by Van Santvoord Merle-Smith. *Courtesy John Hammond.*

According to the account found in a book by Alvin F. Harlow, *Murders Not Quite Solved*, on the morning of September 10, 1931, at around six o'clock in the morning, Captain Harold Howard, a boatman in charge of a yacht at the end of Cove Neck, heard a woman's voice crying for help. Thinking this had to do with a wild party, he went ashore and woke Howard C. Smith's boathouse keeper. Together, they rowed out to the *Bo-Peep*, an open-motor boat belonging to Mr. Smith, which had formerly been used by the New York Yacht Club as a tender for the yacht *Resolute*. There, they found Mrs. Benjamin P. Collings, who proceeded to tell them that during the night, two men had boarded her husband's motorboat, the *Penguin*, and tied him up and thrown him overboard. She said they then put her in a canoe and paddled her to the *Bo-Peep*. Howard C. Smith's boatman, Halvarson, went to the Smith's garage, where a chauffeur, Andrew Cheyne, telephoned Sergeant Forest.

Forest reached the Smith's boathouse around 7:30 a.m., and Mrs. Collings told him her story. She, along with her husband and five-year-old daughter, Barbara, lived on a motorboat called the *Penguin* during the summers. On the night of September 9, they had been in Northport, after which they went to bed. While they were sleeping, two men in a canoe came by and demanded help in getting a wounded man to South Norwalk. Collings refused, as he had no running lights on the *Penguin*. The men came aboard, got Collings to start the boat and run it for some time before they ordered him to stop. At that point, the men from the canoe tied him up and threw him overboard, according to Mrs. Collings, who overheard the scuffle from below decks where she was with her daughter. Then, they left the little girl onboard and took Mrs. Collings to Oyster Bay Harbor and deposited her on the *Bo-Peep*. Mrs. Collings was questioned many times by the Nassau County district attorney, Alvin Edwards, and the Suffolk County assistant district attorney, Fred Munder, without further result.

Mayor Howard C. Smith was reportedly incensed that Mrs. Collings had been turned over to county authorities, as he felt that he had jurisdiction, according to the *Brooklyn Eagle* newspaper. Suffolk Assistant District Attorney Munder conducted a search for the drowned man around the waters of Lloyd Neck with Billy Leeds's yacht. They did not find the body, but they did find five-year-old Barbara safe aboard the *Penguin*, which was towed back to Theodore Roosevelt Memorial Park. Six days later, Benjamin Collings's body washed up on the Caumsett Beach, and on September 29, the body of a man who had been shot in the head was found on Eaton's Neck. This case was never solved, and the reasons for the murders were never discovered.

Robert Forest died in 1962 after a very long career as chief of police. As a tribute to his long service, Cove Neck resident and famed artist Pierre Bourdelle created a weather vane in his honor. Bourdelle was born in Paris, France, in 1903 and was a son of Emil Antoine Bourdelle, a noted sculptor and lifelong friend of Rodin. Pierre joined the faculty at C.W. Post College in 1959 as artist-in-residence. He died in Geneva, Switzerland, on July 7, 1966. The vane portrayed Forest on his motorcycle, along with some friendly squirrels, and was placed on top of the village police booth. It remained there for four or five years before being stolen, which was an extreme embarrassment to the police of the village. No trace of the weather vane has ever been found.

Howard Caswell Smith, the first mayor of Cove Neck, was not related to the Thomas Smith family that had owned the northern part of Cove Neck since they purchased it from Justus Storrs and his wife, Sarah Wright, in 1788. Howard Caswell Smith was born in New York City on February 19, 1871, and was a son of Charles Stewart Smith and Henrietta Haight Caswell. His father's family goes back several generations in Exeter, New

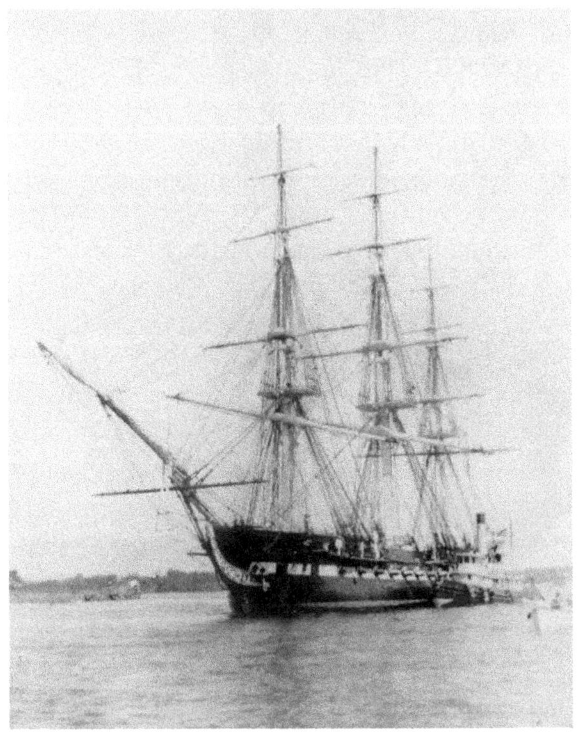

Right: The Village of Cove Neck has had many famous visitors over the years by both land and sea. One of those was the USS *Constitution*, which visited in 1931 as part of its last voyage before being permanently berthed at Charlestown, Massachusetts. *Courtesy John Hammond.*

Below: The second police booth was built alongside the original booth on the land between Cove Neck Road and the bay. *Courtesy John Hammond.*

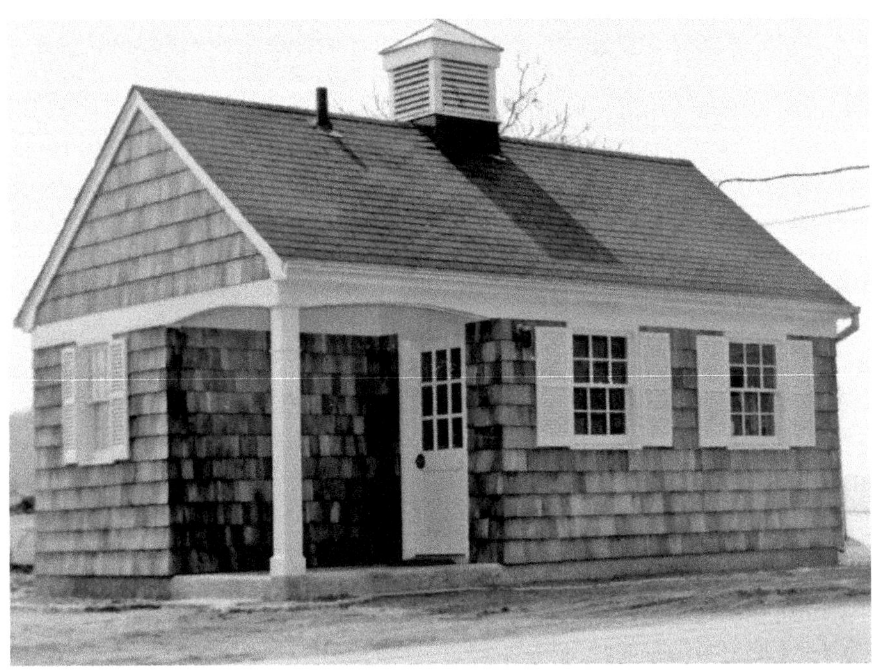

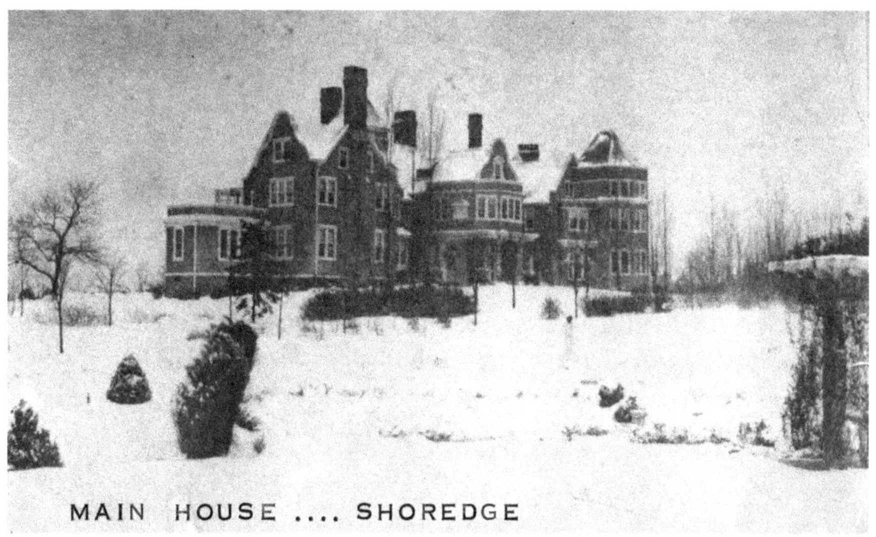

Shoredge was the home of Howard C. Smith, the first mayor of Cove Neck. *Shoredge* was torn down many years ago to build a more modern home. *Courtesy of the Walker family.*

Hampshire. In 1893, Smith graduated from Harvard, where he was the assistant manager of the football team. Immediately following graduation, he began his career in finance, becoming a partner in the Charles Hathaway Company in 1897. He married Katherine Lyall Moen in New York City on October 26, 1898, and, soon thereafter, he purchased property in Cove Neck, where he built a large Tudor-style home in 1906 named *Merry Manor*. He and his wife divorced sometime before World War I, and on December 6, 1919, he married Anna B. Phelps in Washington, D.C. They renamed his estate in Cove Neck to *Shoredge*.

Howard Caswell Smith was elected as the first mayor of Cove Neck and served in this position until 1932, when he was elected as a councilman for the Town of Oyster Bay. After completing his term as councilman, he briefly returned to the position of mayor before Philip James Roosevelt was elected mayor in September 1938. He returned to the position in 1941, following the death of Mayor Philip James Roosevelt, and was reelected for several terms through 1948.

One of the biggest tests for the small village of Cove Neck was when *Sagamore Hill* was proposed as a national shrine, which would change zoning issued by the village. At a hearing in July 1949, all but two of the residents of Cove Neck opposed the Roosevelt Memorial Association's plans to buy *Sagamore Hill* and turn it into a national shrine. The reasons for their opposition included the narrowness of Cove Neck Road, the expected traffic, the expected loss of tax revenue, concerns over rezoning and a fear that visitors would trample their plants and disturb their property, which was, after all, the concern that led to the formation of Cove Neck in 1927. The village turned down the request for a zoning change after prominent residents, including Theodore Roosevelt's cousins John Kean Roosevelt and George Emlen Roosevelt, spoke in opposition.

The Village of Cove Neck continued meeting with representatives from the Roosevelt Memorial Association and the Roosevelt family to try to resolve the situation. While this was going on, the Town of Oyster Bay and Nassau County officials sought ways around the zoning problems associated with the property. The Roosevelt Memorial Association contacted state legislators, which resulted in the introduction of a new bill into the New York State legislature, made to amend the local village law and permit the maintenance of the homes of deceased presidents as memorials by not-for-profit organizations. The bill was signed into law by Governor Thomas E. Dewey and took effect on March 19, 1951, thus making *Sagamore Hill* exempt from the zoning rules of the Incorporated Village of Cove Neck.

On the evening of January 25, 1990, Cove Neck became the center of worldwide attention as the quiet and calm of the small residential

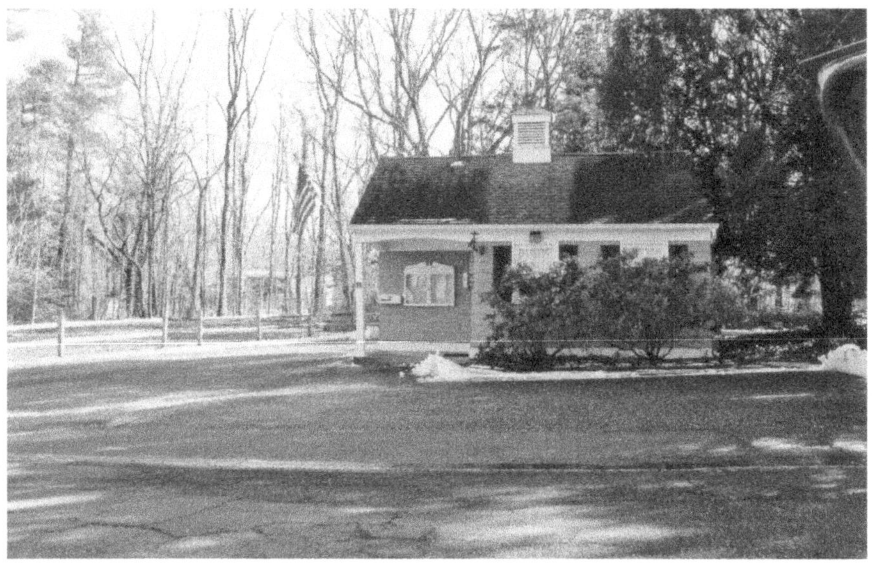

The present police building was built on the arboretum property owned by the Village of Cove Neck. *Courtesy Elizabeth Roosevelt.*

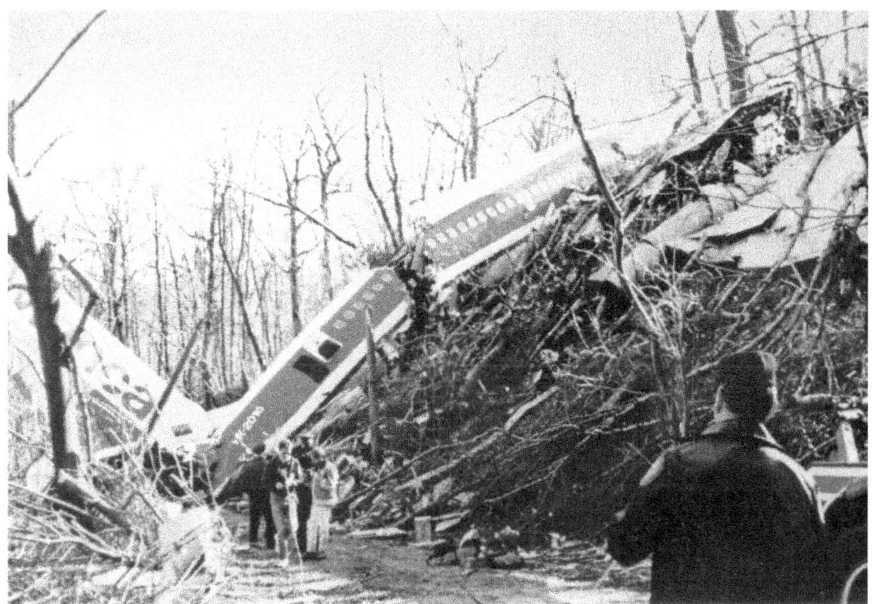

Avianca flight 052 from Colombia, South America, crashed on the evening of January 25, 1990, and put Cove Neck on the news around the world. Here, flight 052 is shown straddling Tennis Court Road. *Courtesy John Hammond.*

community was abruptly disturbed by the crash of Avianca flight 052. Cove Neck resident Rick Robinson was enjoying a quiet evening in his home on Tennis Court Road when he heard something that he later described as the sound of a large truck dropping the blade of a snowplow onto the roadway. When he went outside to investigate, he met Cove Neck policeman Hank LaBella, who had received a communication about a plane crash. They were both expecting to find a small, single-engine private plane but were totally in awe when they discovered a large Boeing 707 lying across Tennis Court Road. The plane had taken off from Colombia, South America, and crashed onto Tennis Court Road while making an approach to Kennedy Airport. Hundreds of first responders, including local firemen and police, descended on the small village to conduct rescue operations. By 2:05 that evening, the last victim was removed, only four and a half hours from the time of the crash. Of the 158 people onboard flight 052, 65 were dead at the scene of the crash, 93 were extricated and transported to local hospitals and 5 of those people later died in hospitals.

16

THE TENNIS COURTS

By Elizabeth Roosevelt

The residents of the village have, in many cases, been tennis players. There was a tennis court at *Sagamore Hill* and one on the property of W. Emlen Roosevelt, across the road from *Sagamore*, in the woods. I believe these were grass courts. I know that the one on the W. Emlen Roosevelt property was destroyed during World War II to become a corn field. The property of Henry H. Anderson also has a tennis court.

The indoor tennis court (which is a club) was founded by families living on Cove Neck. The founding members were Mrs. Henry H. Anderson, George T. Bowdoin, Henry E. Coe Jr., Oliver B. James, George E. Roosevelt, Mrs. Philip J. Roosevelt, Anna L. Straus, Mrs. Alexander White and Mr. and Mrs.

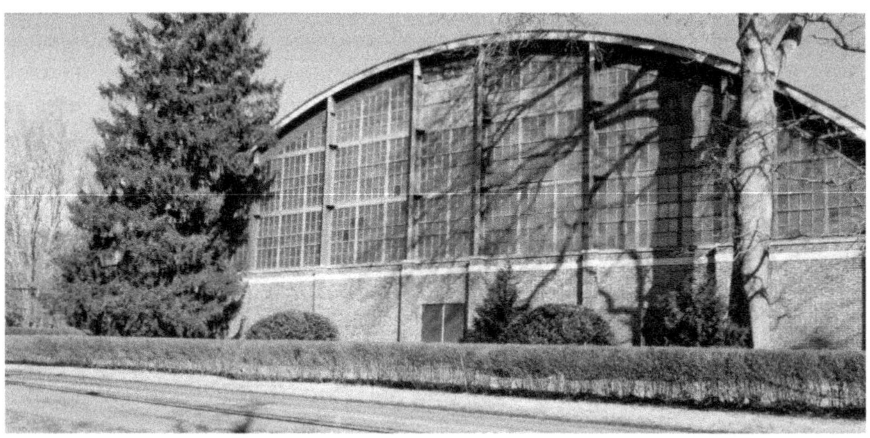

The Tennis Club on Cove Neck Road was built on land donated by the Merle-Smiths. The club later formally bought the land. *Courtesy Elizabeth Roosevelt.*

Van S. Merle-Smith. The club was incorporated on May 28, 1932, and was built on land owned by the Merle-Smiths.

Club membership expanded during the 1930s to include, as it does today, families outside Cove Neck. During World War II, when many members were in the service and gas was rationed, the club's operations were suspended. Due to the efforts of Mrs. Philip J. Roosevelt Jr., the club was reorganized and resumed operations in 1945. At that point, the Roosevelt children and Fritz Coudert were sent to the club to take lessons as a way of getting things started again.

In 1966, the club purchased its property from Mrs. Merle-Smith, and membership increased to the present limit of ninety regular members and sixty-five limited ones.

APPENDIX

In the 1950s, Alfred J. Walker wrote a tribute to the Cove School, which he attended as a young boy. Alfred was the son of Alfred Walker and Mary Moloney, who worked for Mayor Howard C. Smith. His tribute was titled *Christmas Memory* and given to the authors of *Cove Neck: Oyster Bay's Historic Enclave*. Several other family-produced pieces, written by Alfred's nephew Steven Walker, a retired music teacher and former president of the Oyster Bay Historical Society, were also given to the authors of *Cove Neck*.

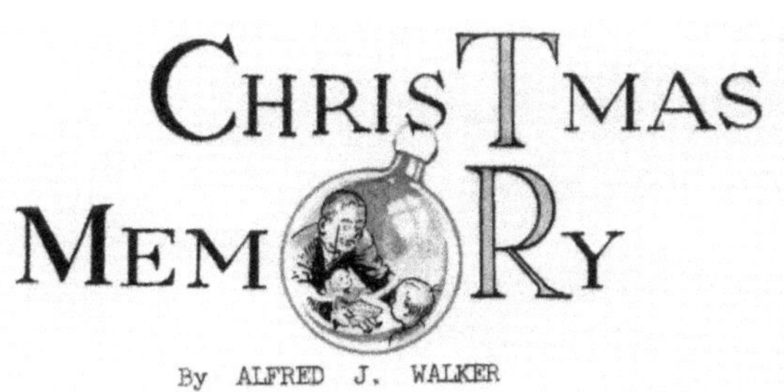

The December day was cold and crisp. Although wintertime more than forty years ago, the sky matched the color of robins' eggs in spring. Snow blanketed the silent woods surrounding *Sagamore Hill*, home of Theodore Roosevelt near the Long Island village of Oyster Bay, New York.

Two miles South, as the Blue-Jay flies, it was the long awaited day of the Christmas Exercises at the Cove School. Annually, the former Rough Rider visited that two room lair of learning and distributed Christmas gifts to the students. His own children had attended the little gray schoolhouse a few years before.

Sleigh bells, in tune to the muted trot of the carriage horses hitched to the ex-president's sleigh, announced the arrival of Theodore Roosevelt and Mrs. Roosevelt at the school. As one of the youngsters assembled in the low ceilinged basement awaiting the arrival of our famous visitor, I was nervous as a tethered pony. With me, about forty "pre-scrubbed and primped-up" schoolmates marched upstairs to our seats on a signal from our faithful teacher, Miss Ella Stewart. I still remember the manner in which T.R. applauded the children, by patting the BACK of his hand. I'm sure his very presence caused a stir amongst the proud parents-to have a world-known personality with them at the Christmas exercises in the role of 'just plain friendly neighbor.'

A large, ornate Christmas tree bedecked the 'performance area' between the two main classrooms of the schoolhouse. A mobile blackboard could be lifted into the ceiling easily with the help of hidden sashweights in the walls. No paper streamers adorned the walls in those days. Instead, lengthy ropes of laurel bordered the blackboards and windows. It was my detail to wield colored chalk and create yuletide motifs.

Simple 'heel and toe' and 1–2–3 dance routines were presented by some youngsters. Story book skits and lengthy recitations were also part of the program. Piano music set the cadence for the 'little folk' dances. At the base of the tinseled Christmas tree, there were gifts 'prechosen' by the children and paid for by the ex-president himself. If memory serves me right, we were allowed a $2 maximum for the checkerboard, jack-knife, doll, 'Parcheesi set', etc. A candy-cone and an orange were accessories accepted with childish relish. Theodore Roosevelt presented the gifts personally to each child. A warm hand-shake went with every present. When six-year old Jimmie O'Neill of the First Grade approached T.R. to receive his gift, a stir of amazement arose when it was evident that the little boy's choice of a present was a DOLL.

Questioned by Theodore Roosevelt as to such a selection, Jimmie explained that his mother had said that God would soon send a baby to the O'Neill cottage. Jimmie chose a doll in case the new baby was a girl. A few days later, Jimmie's mother gave birth to a girl. Now grown to womanhood and married, Jimmie's sister has two sons of her own, one of whom is named Jimmie in honor of the Cove School Jimmie who was killed instantly in a head-on automobile crash on Christmas Eve, 1944, at the age of 32 years.

During those by-gone Decembers, snow covered the roof of the Cove School. Through the closed windows, the voices of the happy children could be heard singing a closing hymn as festivities ended. Memories of those days remain vivid. I recall the last time I saw the former Rough Rider alive. It was an October morning, 1918, three months before his death. At the Cove School, I was outside in the cool autumn morning in a recess group. Down below us, on a grassy shoulder of the Cove Road, Theodore Roosevelt rode by alone on horseback. Beaming that famous smile, he vigorously waved his hand to us and continued on his way-his horse breaking into a slow gallop.

Alfred J. Walker went on to become a noted professional commercial artist and created many local designs, including the Oyster Bay Town Seal, which features a seagull in flight. Alfred created the diagram of the old Cove Schoolhouse, which shows how the rooms were expanded for Theodore Roosevelt's Christmas visits.

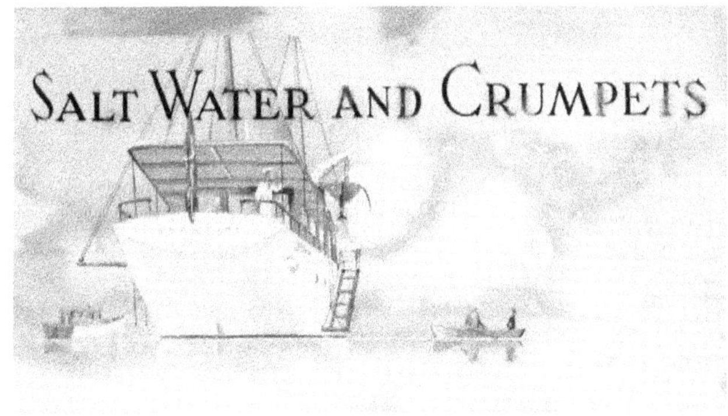

By Alfred J. Walker
Edited by Stephen V. Walker

Drenched with the salt water spray that showered aboard as each white-capped wave was plowed by the plunging bow-stem of the *Aurora* the crew lay prone on the wet, slippery deck. Aloft in the taut rigging of the sleek 47-ton English racing cutter, a slightly audible symphony of the wind could be heard. Clouds, like tumbleweeds in the Heavens, rolled in everchanging formations above the fleet of fifteen racing yachts in the darkening dusk of that by-gone day of August 22, 1851.

At the helm, calculation by compass was all-essential due to the poor visibility of the oncoming night. Binoculars were becoming blind. In the nocturnal dimness on the deck of the *Aurora*, alert crew members would slither to the windward rail and haul in on a straining stay. Among the sailors was one John Walker who, hours before, reluctantly accepted the realization that, in the famous yacht race around the Isle of Wight off England's south coast, the *Aurora*, the smallest boat entered, could only finish as next best.

Far in the lead of the 14 British yachts in that memorable first race for the coveted One Hundred Guineas Cup was the sole Yankee entry, America. A sort of second-hand consolation surged within John when he realized, at least, that there were 13 more unlucky racers wallowing in the wake of the second-place Aurora. Third and fourth places went to the cutters, *Bacchante* and *Eclipse*, respectively. The largest entry, the 392-ton, three masted schooner, *Brilliant*, finished long after midnight in last place. The black-hulled schooner, *America*, had victoriously crossed the finish line at sunset.

Three days later, Queen Victoria went aboard the American yacht to inspect the victorious craft. In officially proclaiming the *America* as winner, Her Royal Highness smilingly conceded that there was no second-place 'runner-up' because the British boats finished so far astern of the fast American schooner. Despite numerous challenges such as the five *Shamrocks* which bloomed from the vast tea fortune of Sir Thomas Lipton, the silver trophy, now known as the America's Cup, rested in the possession of Uncle Sam for 131 years, the greatest winning streak in sports history, until it was finally broken in 1983 by skipper John Bertrand's *Australia II*.

Like the clouds, a few years rolled by and John, the *Aurora* sailor, married his lovely Isle of Wight sweetheart, Charlotte Gutteridge. They made their home in the picturesque, garden-strewn hamlet of Seaview. Six children, two girls and four boys, enlarged the 'tot crew' in the Walker cottage on Salterns Road. After first-born James, the second child, Blanche Amy, born March 28, 1863, was destined to out-live all of her brothers and sisters. But though she lived to the ripe age of 94 years, she knew widowhood for sixty-two years, losing her sailor husband to illness in 1895. Like the guiding beam in the lighthouse near her Coast Guard cottage in Cuckmere Haven, Amy's light shone for eight little ones as they gazed on the brilliance of the chalk white Seven Sisters.

The youngest child of Charlotte and John Walker, born February 4, 1872, was christened Alfred Henry. Like his sister, Emily, and his brother, William, he emigrated to America, at the turn of the new century. He married an Irish colleen, Mary Moloney, who had sailed to the United States from County Tipperary. They found work as caretaker and servant at a lovely seaside estate on Long Island's north shore. Two sons were born to Alfred and Mary, the younger being the author. The two brothers eventually married two sisters, each having three boys apiece, close in age, and doubly close as cousins.

My sailor grandfather, John Walker, died when my father was a boy on the Isle of Wight. But my grandmother Charlotte sheltered her brood of six ably as the youngsters grew into adolescence. Fond memories of my father's boyhood in Seaview were shared by his best friend and school chum, one Newton Jones. At the quaint school house or on the soccer meadow nearby, Newton and Alf were inseparable. After chore time, when geraniums were watered and garden weeds disposed of, Alf would be rewarded with his Mum's delicious crumpets. He would save some for Newton. Adventurous beach-combing trips were made more enjoyable for the two lads when one of Alf's pockets bulged with Mum's crumpets.

One sunny afternoon, long, long ago, the two pals decided to go fishing from their favorite rock jetty that jutted out into the wind-churned Solent. The sky, the color of robins' eggs, was flecked with white, drifting clouds. In the imaginative minds of the boys, the clouds seemed to take on all sorts of shapes, from a far-away polar bear to white mounds of Mum's dumplings. While nibbling crumpets, the two ten-year old explorers waited like sentinels for tell-tale tugs on their fish lines.

Far off in the distance, the sound of hoof beats on the narrow shorefront road became more and more audible. In glistening harness, high-stepping carriage horses of a Royal entourage trotted towards the boys' lair. In one of the carriages was Queen Victoria, an older monarch than the young Queen who inspected the *America* years before. The destination of the approaching caravan was *Osborne House*, the Queen's elite showplace in East Cowes designed by her beloved Albert, where a formal function awaited the elderly Queen's arrival. To avoid the crowds assembled along the main route to Cowes, the coachmen were ordered to follow the less populated route at Seaview. Trained to respect Royalty as they were trained to respect parents and elders, Alfred and Newton stood at attention at the side of the road after scurrying shoreward over the rocks of the jetty. As Queen Victoria passed in her carriage she graciously acknowledged the two young boys by bowing to them as she waved her handkerchief. Repeatedly, during the rest of their lives, Alfred and Newton proudly described the Queen's gesture.

When in later years, Alfred left the Isle of Wight to sail to America; he knew the remorse of saying farewell to his mother, sister and brothers who stayed in England. To also say goodbye to good friend Newton Jones was also an ordeal. However, new adventures called to him in the New World. He found his joy and livelihood in horticulture. As gardener and caretaker of *Shoredge*, the seaside estate of Col. Howard C. Smith on the tip of Cove Neck in Oyster Bay, New York, he afforded my brother and me a wonderful boyhood in picturesque Long Island countryside.

And like my father before me, there were brushes with American "royalty" for down the road from the sprawling *Shoredge* was *Sagamore Hill*, home of ex-president Theodore Roosevelt. One day when I was out rowing on the harbor with my father, the famous Rough Rider was heard to call out, "I see you're starting him nice and young, Mr. Walker." And at Christmastime, when President and Mrs. Roosevelt came to visit the Cove School, I had the honor of drawing yuletide motifs on the chalkboard. Vivid memories of the great man linger on, and especially his advice, "Keep your eyes on the stars but keep your feet on the ground," and "Walk softly but carry a big stick." Teddy's broad, toothsome grin was as familiar as his favorite bellowed expression of approval, "Bully!" My favorite quote of T.R. is "When you come to the end of your rope tie a knot and hang on!"

In 1921 when I reached the age of thirteen, a memorable revelation unfolded out on the harbor soon after dawn one September morning. I yawningly awoke to see that a U.S. Navy boat had anchored overnight off the Seawanhaka Corinthian Yacht Club directly across the bay from *Shoredge*. On the gray bow of the World War I Sub-Chaser, the morning light revealed the large white numerals 208. Hove to alongside the Navy boat was the black hull of the original racing schooner, *America* in tow of the Sub-Chaser and, without masts or bow-sprit, the famous hull was enroute from Boston Harbor to the U.S. Naval Academy at Annapolis.

My father and I dressed with the speed of firemen, by-passed breakfast, and jogged down across the eight-acre lawn to the boat house beyond the 35-room main mansion on *Shoredge*. Inquisitive as cats, we extracted a small varnished dingy from the boat house and rowed out to have a look at the real *America*. The Navy officer in charge invited us aboard. On

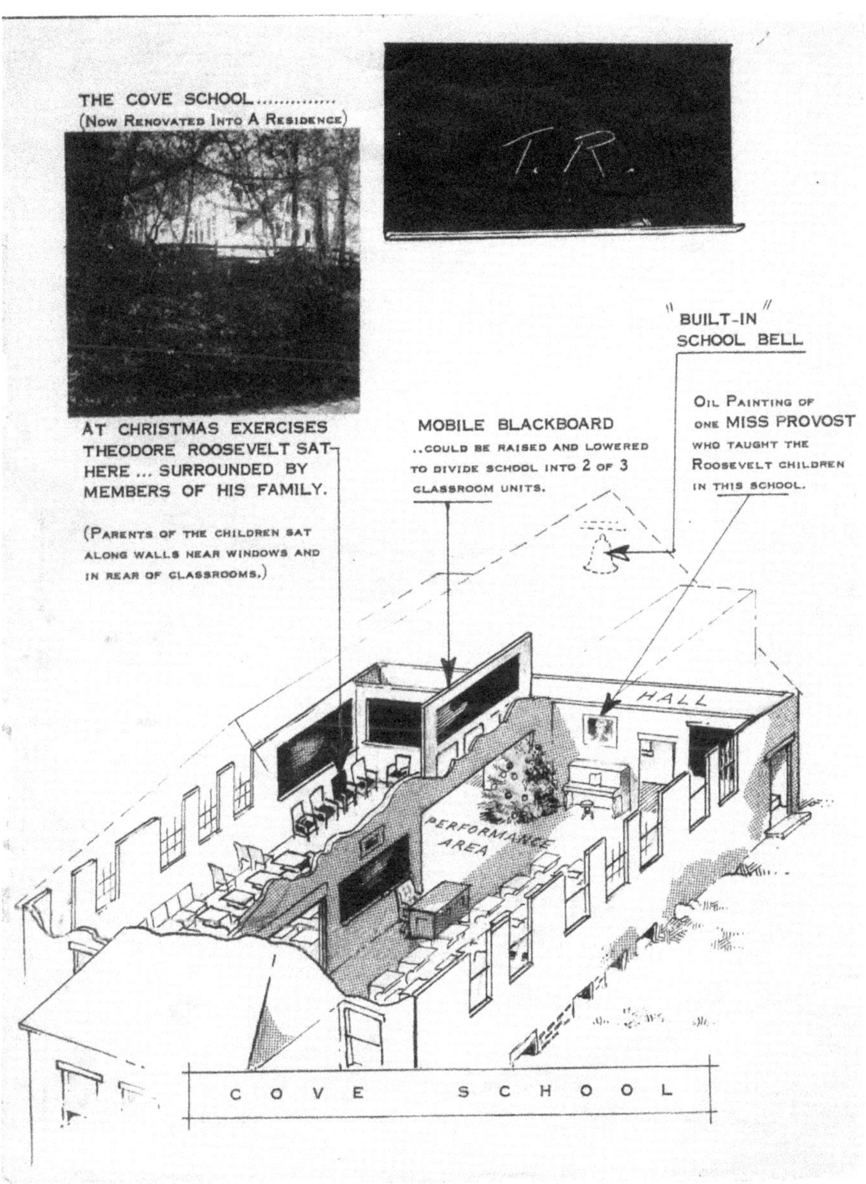
THE COVE SCHOOL..............
(Now Renovated Into A Residence)
T. R.
"BUILT-IN" SCHOOL BELL
AT CHRISTMAS EXERCISES THEODORE ROOSEVELT SAT HERE ... SURROUNDED BY MEMBERS OF HIS FAMILY.
(Parents of the children sat along walls near windows and in rear of classrooms.)
MOBILE BLACKBOARD ..could be raised and lowered to divide school into 2 or 3 classroom units.
Oil Painting of one MISS PROVOST who taught the Roosevelt children in this school.
HALL
PERFORMANCE AREA
COVE SCHOOL

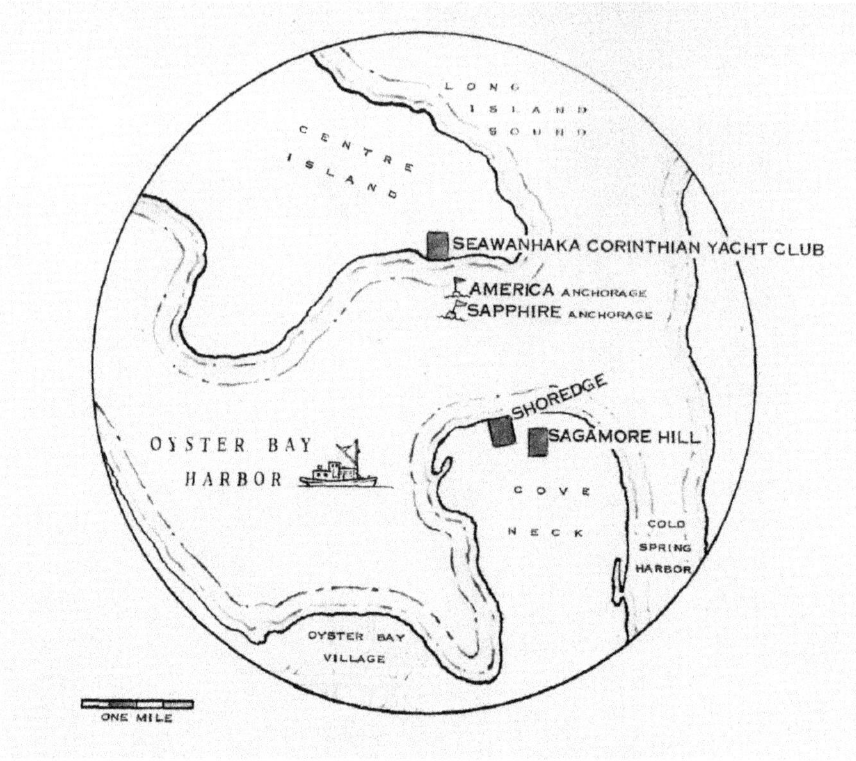

deck, when my father related that his father sailed on the *Aurora* against the *America* in the original One Hundred Guineas Cup, we were given a section of the America's main-sail stop as a souvenir.

Four years later, the same varnished dingy was used again by my father and me when we rowed out on the harbor to get a closer look at a huge, gleaming white steam yacht that had dropped anchor off the Seawanhaka Corinthian Yacht Club. The big beautiful clipper-bow yacht was the *Saffire* from the Royal Yacht Squadron of Cowes, England. Letters from Aunt Amy had alerted us that her nephew, and likewise, my father's nephew, a Stanley Walker, would be aboard the *Sapphire* as a young steward. Stanley was the son of Amy and Alfred's brother Charles.

When our dingy with its crew of two, my father and me, reached the high stern of the British yacht, a bearded, middle-aged sailor waved down to us and called out a jolly, "Ahoy, there." My father asked the bearded one if there was a Stanley Walker on board in the crew and, with thick Cockney accent, the old sailor assured us that there was a 'Walker' below decks but he was not certain as to the first name, Stanley.

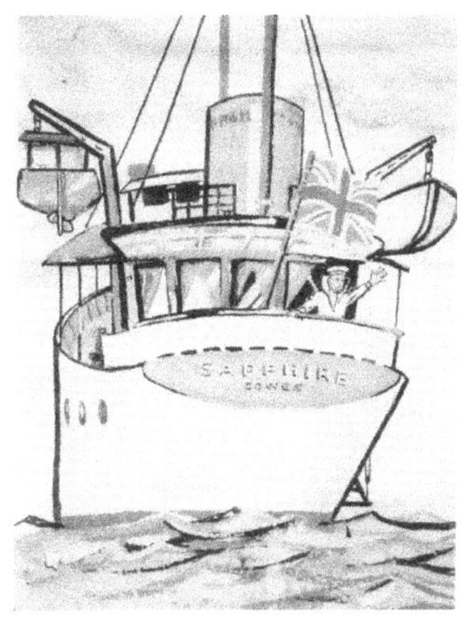

This saga of the sea ends with an amazing revelation which Cousin Stanley, indeed on board, was prompted to relay. We entertained him ashore at our cottage on the Smith estate for three days until the big yacht sailed. Listening to Stanley's descriptions, my father tried to piece together the old village he knew years before as a child with Stanley's portrait of the modern Seaview. My father then asked his nephew if he knew whatever became of a Newton Jones, his old friend and school chum. With a twinkle in his eyes, Stanley enlightened my soon-to-be astonished father that the bearded middle-aged sailor who greeted us from the high stern of the *Sapphire* was none other than Newton Jones.

THE LADY SCHOONERS

By Mary M. Walker

The sailing sloops flying mastheads from distant ports of call majestically lay at anchor off the coast at Sand City in the early years of the twentieth century as Cove Neck's barons proudly displayed their view of the picturesque harbor. But it is the hard working schooners who plied their slow and heavy burden from Brooklyn to the estates and back again that I have become most interested in. Indeed it is the work of the *Sarah Quinn*, the *Ella B. Simpson* and similar craft which made the life of the landed gentry as enviable and luxurious as it was in the 1910's and 20's.

These broad-of-beam working schooners were two-masted affairs, approximately seventy feet in length, with plenty of room above decks to contain enough coal, bricks, sand or manure to carry an estate like that of Colonel Howard C. Smith or Mr. E.F. Whitney through the fall or spring months. Manure incidentally, was a much valued item at that time and not enough could be obtained locally despite the horse and cattle population of Long Island. Now, Brooklyn, that was another matter. Brooklyn had too much manure from its endless horse barns all up and down Montague Street. It was a profitable business indeed for a captain to load up the *Louise* with the forerunner of Agrico and take it out to the Colonel's estate, *Shoredge*, providing winds and tides were cooperative. One can speculate on the restlessness of that crew of three or four men aboard the *Louise* as they sometimes lagged along in calm waters tacking back and forth with her pungent freight, past Hell Gate, Bowery Bay, out along the East River, past City Island and Hart Island in the Sound and on out to Oyster Bay Harbor. The trip would last all day.

Upon arrival at Oyster Bay, the captain and his crew would raise the centerboard and then maneuver his way up onto the beach as far as the high tide would float him. These schooners had a tough rounded bottom which adapted nicely to being deposited up on the beach. Then after the anchor was dropped, they awaited the coming of the ebb tide so their cargo could be unloaded.

In the meantime preparations had been made on shore to help disburden the vessel. The Colonel had hired a local contractor with three or four teams of horses and farm carts to accomplish this. Depending on the slope of the beach and the tide, the unloading could be accomplished in two hours on the ebb tide and two hours on the flood tide. Horses could still perform their job with water up to their knees. It was no easy task to pull the heavy loads up out of the water, through the grinding sand and up to the barns. Later the manure had to be carefully placed on each square foot of the asparagus beds as well as the spacious lawn which ran from the big house to the beach. To this day the lawn shows the special nutritive diet it has historically received.

Most of the coal that was brought out to Oyster Bay was loaded on at Perth Amboy, New Jersey. On the return trip Captain Jeremiah Lunch might carry a load of gravel on the *Sarah Quinn*. Another loading point was Lloyd's Neck where such cargoes as bricks from W.K. Hammond were important. *The Messenger*, captained by Charlie Van Dyke, set sail from Lloyd's Neck and headed for West Farms. Captain Jack Connell, who later piloted the Bayles' oyster boats for over fifty years, got his first experiences as a sailor of fifteen on the *Messenger*. The captain and crew had to be good sailors to make the long and tedious trips back and forth to Brooklyn. It helped too if you could play a good hand of pinochle.

Life aboard the schooners was completely absorbing to young boys whose fathers were employed on the estates of Cove Neck. Living on

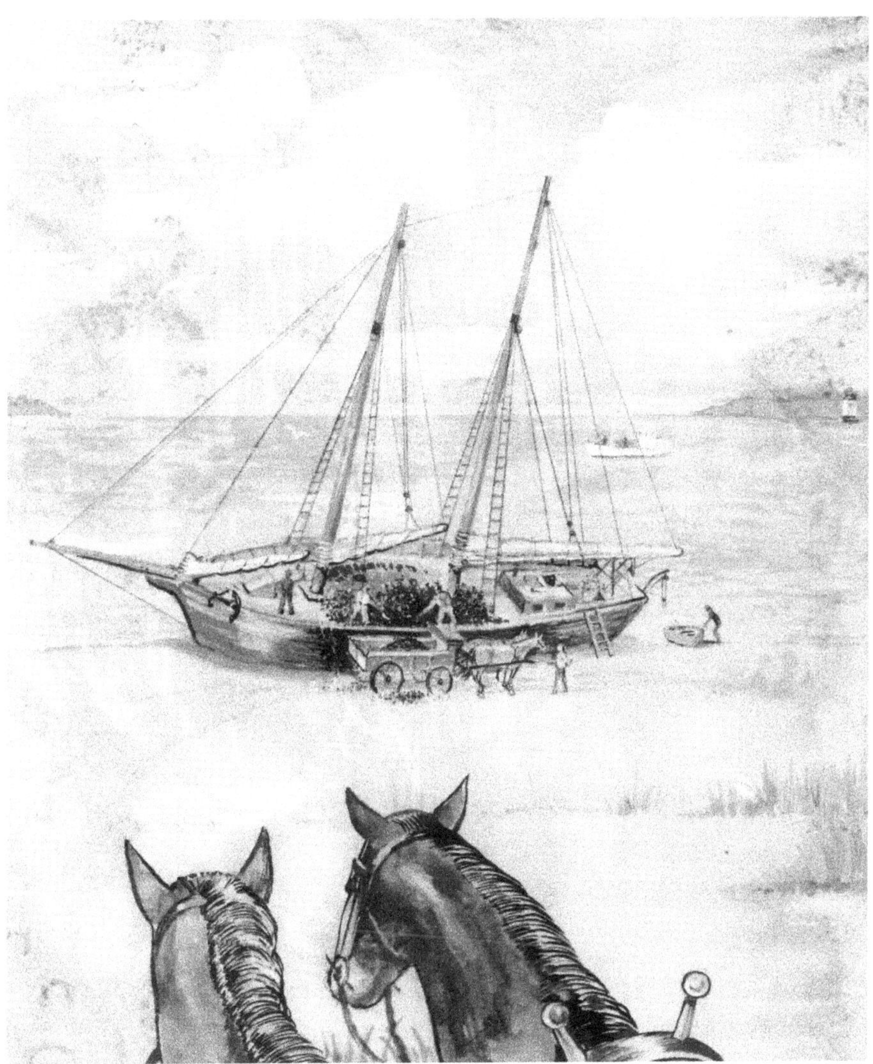

Howard C. Smith's estate Dan and Alfred Walker often saw the colorful schooners arrive and depart. They climbed aboard the old vessels and saw the crew at work and at play. They watched Frank Faraco's teams of horses pull their heavy loads of coal over the sand and up to the barns. Then after the tide had lifted the hulk of the *Mary Buckley*, she would ease away from the shore toward the horizon. The water washed away the deep ruts the wagons had made. The only reminders of the whole incident were a few pieces of coal high up on beach.

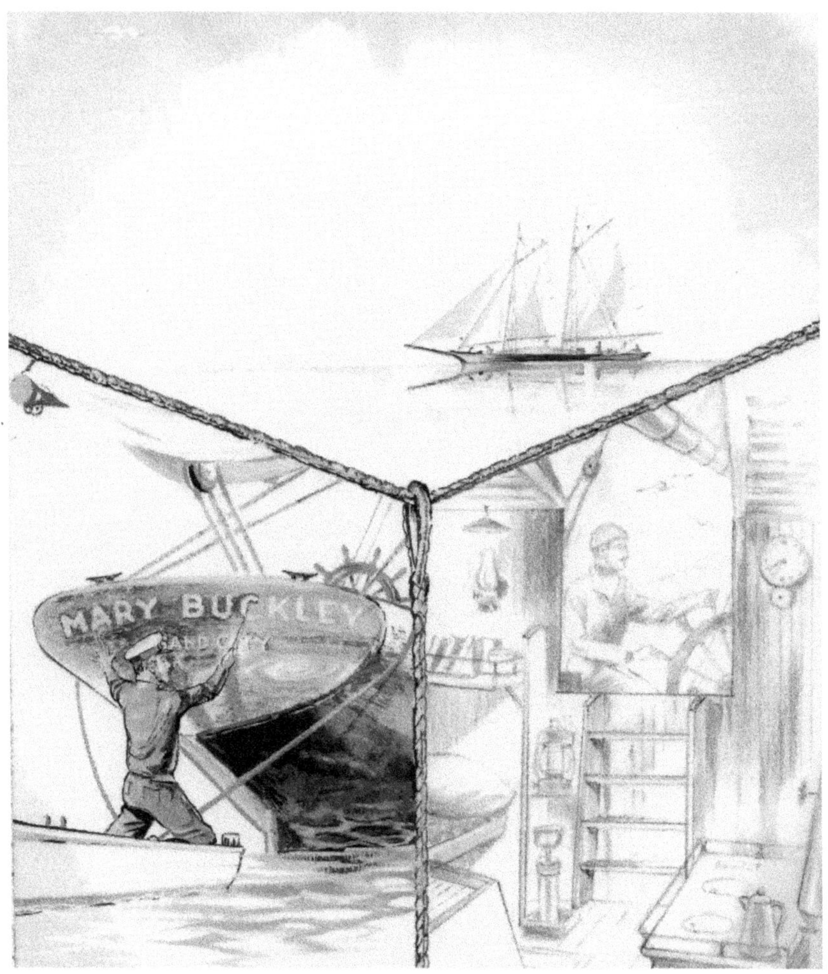

The era of the sailing, working schooner gave way to the steam, gasoline and later diesel powered vessels. But one enjoys reflecting on those colorful 'sea horses' of the early twentieth century with their maidenly names: the *Emma Sutherland*, the *Margaret Anne* and the *Fanny Fowler*. They were famous long before it became fashionable to name hurricanes after the ladies.

Mary M. Walker was an English teacher and librarian in the Oyster Bay Schools. Mary Walker was the mother of Steven Walker, a former music teacher at Oyster Bay High School.

The accompanying illustrations were made by Alfred J. Walker, artist and uncle of Steven Walker.

BIBLIOGRAPHY

Angel, Rabbi Marc D. *Remnant of Israel: A Portrait of America's First Jewish Congregation—Shearith Israel*. New York: Riverside Book Company, 2004.

Ben-Jacob, Michael. *Nathan Simson: A Biographical Sketch of a Colonial Jewish Merchant*. New York: American Jewish Archives Journal, 1999.

Bleyer, Bill. *Sagamore Hill: Theodore Roosevelt's Summer White House*. Charleston, SC: The History Press, 2016.

Brooklyn Daily Eagle. November 14, 1858, September 11, 1911, February 6, 1927, December 19, 1929, February 2, 1930.

Colonial History & Minutes of Town Meetings 1736–1791. Westchester County, New York, 1975. North Castle/New Castle Historical Records.

Cooper, Mary Wright. *The Diary of Mary Cooper: Life on a Long Island Farm 1768–1773*. New York: Publishing Center for Cultural Resources, 1981.

Cove Neck Village Archives.

Cowles, Anna Roosevelt. *Letters from Theodore Roosevelt to Anna Roosevelt Cowles 1870–1918*. New York: Charles Scribner's Sons, 1924.

Cox, George W. *Oyster Bay Town Records*. Vol. 1 *1653–1690*. New York: Tobias A. Wright, 1916.

Dalton, Kathleen. *Theodore Roosevelt: A Strenuous Life*. New York: Alfred A. Knopf, 2002.

East Norwich Enterprise. Microfilm Records. Oyster Bay East Norwich Public Library. Oyster Bay, NY.

Gable, John Allen, ed. *The Roosevelt Family in America a Genealogy, Theodore Roosevelt Association Journal* 16, no. 1–3 (1990). Oyster Bay, NY: Privately printed.

Griffin, Thomas. Family papers and photographs.

Hammond, John Edward. *Crossroads: A History of East Norwich*. Privately printed, 1997.

———. *Matinecock Light: The History of Matinecock Lodge No. 806*. Huntington, NY: Maple Hill Press, 1992.

———. *Oyster Bay Remembered*. Huntington, NY: Maple Hill Press, 2002.

———. *When the Sirens Sound*. Huntington, NY: Maple Hill Press, 1996.

Irvin, Frances. *Oyster Bay: A Sketch Revised by Jane Soames Nickerson*: Mattituck, NY: Amereon Ltd., 1987.

Johnston, William Davison, and Richard W. Reifsnyder. *A Pilgrimage of Faith: The History of the First Presbyterian Church Oyster Bay, New York*. Huntington, NY: Maple Hill Press, 1990.

———. *Oyster Bay in History: A Sketch*. Oyster Bay, NY: Privately printed, 1960.

Jones, John H. *The Jones Family of Long Island: Descendants of Major Thomas Jones*. New York: Tobias A. Wright, 1907.

MacKay, John F., ed. *Walls Have Tongues: Oyster Bay Buildings and Their Stories*. Oyster Bay, NY: Oyster Bay Historical Society, 1977.

Merle-Smith, Van S. Jr. *The Village of Oyster Bay: Its Founding and Growth From 1653 to 1700*. Garden City, NY: Privately printed, 1953.

Morison, Elting E., ed. *The Letters of Theodore Roosevelt*. Cambridge, MA: Harvard University Press, 1951.

Morris, Sylvia Jukes. *Edith Kermit Roosevelt: Portrait of a First Lady*. New York: Vintage Books, 1990.

Mowrer, Lilian T. *The Indomitable John Scott, Citizen of Long Island 1632–1704*. New York: Farrar, Strauss and Cudahy, 1960.

Munsell, W.W. *History of Queens County, New York*. New York: W.W. Munsell & Co., 1882.

New York Times. January 3, 1972.

Oyster Bay Guardian. Microfilm copies. Oyster Bay East Norwich Public Library. Oyster Bay, NY.

Oyster Bay Historical Society. *An Upstairs, Downstairs Look at Oyster Bay Estate Life*. Oyster Bay, NY: Oyster Bay Historical Society, 2005.

———. *Recreation During the 20th Century in Oyster Bay*. Oyster Bay, NY: Oyster Bay Historical Society, 2002.

Oyster Bay Historical Society Archives.

Peck, William. Oyster Bay Properties, Vertical files. Oyster Bay Historical Society.

Pennypacker, Morton. *General Washington's Spies on Long Island and in New York.* Garden City, NY: Country Life Press Corporation, 1939.

———. *The Two Spies Nathan Hale and Robert Townsend.* New York: Houghton Mifflin Company, 1930.

Perrine, Howland Delano. *The Wright Family of Oyster Bay.* New York: Privately printed, 1923.

Robinson, Corinne Roosevelt. *My Brother Theodore Roosevelt.* New York: Charles Scribner's Sons, 1921.

Roosevelt, Theodore. *Theodore Roosevelt, An Autobiography.* New York: Charles Scribner's Sons, 1913. Reprint, Boston: Da Capo Press, 1985.

Savage, James. *A Genealogical Dictionary of the First Settlers of New England.* Boston: Little, Brown and Company, 1860.

Smits, Edward J. *Nassau Suburbia, USA.* Garden City, NY: Doubleday & Company, 1974.

Tallmadge, Col. Benjamin. *Memoir, Prepared by Himself at the Request of His Children.* New York: Thomas Holman, 1858.

Times-Picayune. November 26, 1858.

Townsend, Charlotte A. *Memorial of John, Henry, and Richard Townsend.* New York: W.A. Townsend, 1865.

Trimble, Marian Blackton. *J. Stuart Blackton: A Personal Biography by His Daughter.* Metuchen, NJ: The Scarecrow Press, 1985.

Youngs, Daniel Kelsey. *Oyster Bay Youngs Record.* Jamaica, NY: Charles Welling, 1890.

Youngs, Mary Fanny. Narrative to her nieces, 1948, unpublished in author's collection.

——— . *When We Were Little: Children's Rhymes of Oyster Bay.* New York: E.P. Dutton & Company, 1919. Reprint, Oyster Bay, NY: Oyster Bay Historical Society, 1985.

Youngs, Selah, Jr. *Youngs Family.* New York: Privately printed, 1907.

ABOUT THE AUTHORS

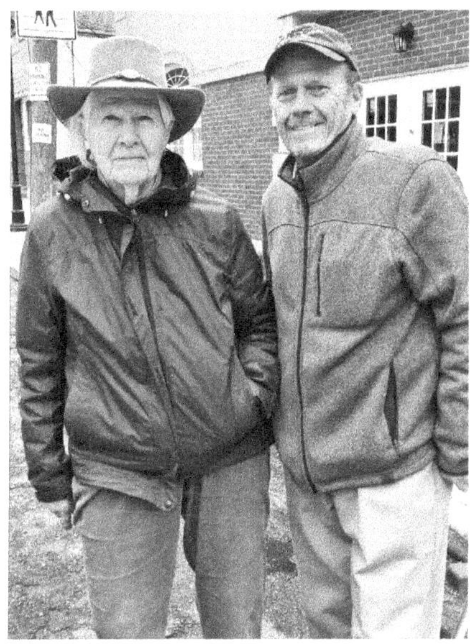

Elizabeth Emlen Roosevelt is the official historian for the Incorporated Village of Cove Neck, where she has resided for many years. Liz, as she is known locally, is a first cousin twice removed of President Theodore Roosevelt. She is a longtime member of the Theodore Roosevelt Association and currently serves as assistant treasurer of the organization. She taught history for thirty-two years, beginning with four years at Syosset (New York) High School, then one year at a school in Hastings, New Zealand, and, finally, twenty-seven years at Friends Academy in Locust Valley, New York. Miss Roosevelt earned a bachelor's degree in history from the University of Denver and a master's degree in history from Long Island University. She is a member of Seawanhaka Corinthian Yacht Club and an active competitive sailor. In her spare time, Miss Roosevelt volunteers for the Oyster Bay Historical Society as the manager of its gift shop in the Earle-Wightman House Museum.

John Edward Hammond is the official historian for the Township of Oyster Bay. Mr. Hammond is a lifelong resident of Oyster Bay, where some of his ancestors settled in 1653. He earned a bachelor's degree from the University of the State of New York and is a graduate of Yale University's Institute of Far Eastern Languages. He proudly served in the United States Air Force Security Service from 1964 to 1968. He is the author of five books: *Matinecock Light* (1992), *Crossroads: A History of East Norwich* (1997), *When the Sirens Sound* (1996), *Oyster Bay Remembered* (2002) and *Oyster Bay*, Images of America (2009). He has also researched and authored four genealogical research guides: *Historic Cemeteries of Oyster Bay*, *Index to Register of Deaths (1881–1920)*, *Birth, Marriage and Death Records (1847–1849)* and *Civil War Records: Town of Oyster Bay*. Mr. Hammond is an avid golfer who occasionally shoots his age.

www.ingramcontent.com/pod-product-compliance
Lightning Source LLC
LaVergne TN
LVHW052337100826
845147LV00020B/1098

* 9 7 8 1 4 6 7 1 4 4 3 7 7 *